Teilhard's Mysticism

Teilhard's Mysticism

Seeing the Inner Face of Evolution

Kathleen Duffy, SSJ

ORBIS BOOKS

Maryknoll, New York 10545

ORBIS BOOKS
Maryknoll, New York 10545

Fathers and Brothers
MARYKNOLL.

Founded in 1970, Orbis Books endeavors to publish works that enlighten the mind, nourish the spirit, and challenge the conscience. The publishing arm of the Maryknoll Fathers and Brothers, Orbis seeks to explore the global dimensions of the Christian faith and mission, to invite dialogue with diverse cultures and religious traditions, and to serve the cause of reconciliation and peace. The books published reflect the views of their authors and do not represent the official position of the Maryknoll Society. To learn more about Maryknoll and Orbis Books, please visit our website at www.maryknollsociety.org.

Manufactured in the United States of America.
Manuscript editing and typesetting by Joan Weber Laflamme.

Library of Congress Cataloging-in-Publication Data

. Duffy, Kathleen, 1941–
  Teilhard's mysticism : seeing the inner face of evolution / Kathleen Duffy, SSJ.
      pages cm
  Includes bibliographical references and index.
  ISBN 978-1-62698-085-3
      1. Teilhard de Chardin, Pierre. 2. Christian biography. 3. Mysticism. I. Title.
BX4705.T39D84 2014
230'.2092—dc23

2014003755

Contents

Acknowledgments

Many persons have helped to make this book possible. I would particularly like to thank the administration at Chestnut Hill College for providing me with a sabbatical year to begin this project and subsequent release time to complete it. I am grateful to several prominent Teilhard scholars—John Haught, Ursula King, the late Thomas King, SJ, John Grim, Mary Evelyn Tucker, Ilia Delio, and James Salmon, SJ—whose writings about Teilhard have inspired me and whose friendship, support, and encouragement have sustained my efforts. My interaction with members of the Board of the American Teilhard Association, particularly as editor of *Teilhard Studies*, the Association's biannual publication, has also helped to broaden my insights into Teilhard's work. Those who read earlier versions of this manuscript—John Haught, Ursula King, and John Grim—have suggested important improvements. Several of my colleagues and friends have read all or part of the manuscript in its many stages, have made useful comments, and have encouraged me to publish. I am particularly grateful to Mary Steinmetz, Liz Sweeney, SSJ, Edward Devinney, Pat Marnien, SSJ, Aida Beaupied, Margie Thompson, SSJ, and Rosemary Parkinson. A special note of thanks goes to Marcy Springer, SSJ, who offered me the peace and comfort of her retreat center, Francis House of Prayer, when I needed a quiet place to work. I would also like to thank Robert Ellsberg, Maria Angelini, and the staff at Orbis Books who have brought this book to publication. Finally, I am grateful to Teilhard, who continues to inspire me and whose worldview continues to enrich my life.

Foreword

Christianity today, not for the first time, is in crisis. Many former Catholics and other Christians are looking outside the churches for a religious home—that is, if they haven't abandoned the spiritual search altogether. There are many reasons for this disillusionment, but I think the problem is at least partly metaphysical. It has to do with a whole world-view that no longer rings true for many thoughtful people. Educated seekers often find in the churches a spirituality out of step with current science, especially evolutionary biology, physics, and the new cosmology. At the same time, many religious believers are suffocated by the soul-deadening scientism of so much contemporary academic culture.

Both Christian traditionalism and current scientific naturalism foster ways of looking at the world that have the effect of "clipping the wings of hope," as Pierre Teilhard de Chardin would have put it. Hope needs a lofty horizon, one that reaches beyond personal existence, human history, and the universe itself. Early Christian apocalyptic literature, along with the Pauline letters to the Romans, Colossians, and Ephesians, expressed a longing to stretch Christian expectation so that it covers the whole of creation. Likewise today, if faith is to bring healing and hope, it needs to be clothed in the raiment of deep time, cosmic immensity, and the story of nature's emergent complexity.

Human existence, as science has taught us, is tied to a fourteen-billion-year-old cosmic drama—and possibly to a multiverse. Any faith tradition that fails to link up with this wider-than-human world cannot satisfy enlightened minds and hearts. Understandably, many educated people now breathe more deeply within the expansive universe of scientific discovery than they do in church. For them, science is sufficient and nature enough. Their true spiritual masters are Darwin, Einstein, and Hawking. An expanding physical universe, not priests, popes, or theologians, has set them free.

Or has it? Can science alone give us a world big enough to relieve our native restlessness? Does science divorced from mysticism fully satisfy our unquiet hearts or our boundless curiosity? Many honest people would answer affirmatively, and no doubt for them nature is spiritually adequate. For Teilhard and his astute interpreter Kathleen Duffy, however, a pure naturalism, no matter how extensively it rescales the universe in space, time, and complexity, is not enough. Scientism is no less confining than a religious piety that ignores the cosmos.

Kathleen Duffy has witnessed to her love of nature in her thirty-five-year-long career as a professor of physics. Yet her enlightened grasp of the universe's temporal depth, spatial breadth, and lavish beauty still leaves her restless. She wants something more, indeed infinitely more. She finds it, or at least an opening to it, in Teilhard's exceptional synthesis of Christian mysticism and scientific awareness. Unfortunately, the great Jesuit scientist's original ideas, though more relevant today than ever, seldom get more than passing mention in schools of theology, seminaries, or suburban pulpits. Readers, however, will find in Duffy's jewel of a book a rich and reliable guide to the Teilhardian vision that many of us have found to be both religiously healing and intellectually satisfying in the age of science.

The author realizes that all of us, especially the scientifically educated, need an understanding of God that is larger than the universe. As Teilhard often complained, the God of our churches is too small. Their "fixist" spirituality no longer fits the dynamic cosmos that the natural sciences are now laying out so lavishly. Like Teilhard, the author of this evocative work feels the need to expand our sense of the divine in proportion to the new horizons of science. The task is more pressing than ever. What scientists and people of faith need, as Teilhard wrote in 1919, is a God "as vast and mysterious as the Cosmos." He adds: "A God who made the World less mysterious, or smaller, or less important to us, than our heart and reason show it to be, that God–less beautiful than the God we await–will never more be (One) to whom the Earth kneels" (HM, 212). Teilhard, therefore, would take great delight in the pages you are about to read.

JOHN F. HAUGHT

Georgetown University

Abbreviations for Works by Teilhard de Chardin

A   *Activation of Energy: Enlightening Reflections on Spiritual Energy.* Translated by René Hague. New York: A Harvest Book/Harcourt, 1978.

B   *Building the Earth.* Translated by Nöel Lindsay. Wilkes-Barre, PA: Dimension Books, 1965.

C   *Christianity and Evolution.* Translated by René Hague. New York: Harcourt Brace Jovanovich, 1969.

D   *The Divine Milieu.* New York: Harper and Row, 1960.

F   *The Future of Man.* Translated by Norman Denny. New York: Harper and Row, 1964.

HE   *Human Energy.* Translated by J. M. Cohen. New York: Harcourt Brace Jovanovich, 1969.

HM   *The Heart of Matter.* Translated by René Hague. New York: Harcourt Brace Jovanovich, 1978.

HP   *The Human Phenomenon.* Translated by Sara Appleton-Weber. Portland OR: Sussex Academic Press, 1999.

HU   *Hymn of the Universe.* Translated by Simon Bartholomew. New York: Harper and Row, 1961.

J   *Journal*, Tome I, August 26, 1915–January 4, 1919. Unabridged text published by Nicole and Karl Schmitz-Moormann. Paris: Fayard, 1975.

LJM   *Lettres à Jeanne Mortier.* Paris: Éditions du Seuil, 1984.

LLZ   *Letters to Léontine Zanta.* New York: Harper and Row,
        1968.

LT   *Letters from a Traveler.* New York: Harper and Row, 1962.

LTF   *Letters to Two Friends 1926–1952.* Translated by Helen
        Weaver and edited by Ruth Nanda Anshen. New York:
        New American Library, 1967.

MM   The *Making of a Mind: Letters from a Soldier-Priest
        1941–1919.* Translated by René Hague. New York: Harper
        and Row, 1965.

S   *Science and Christ.* Translated by René Hague. New York:
        Harper and Row, 1968.

T   *Towards the Future.* Translated by René Hague. New York:
        Harcourt Brace Jovanovich, 1975.

V   *The Vision of the Past.* Translated by J. M. Cohen. New
        York: Harper and Row, 1966.

W   *Writings in Time of War.* Translated by René Hague. New
        York: Harper and Row, 1968.

Introduction

The Diaphany of the Divine at the heart of a glowing Universe, as I have experienced it through contact with Earth—
the Divine radiating from the depths of a blazing Matter:
this it is that I shall try to disclose and communicate in what follows.

—Pierre Teilhard de Chardin,
Heart of Matter, 16

Jesuit paleontologist Pierre Teilhard de Chardin has developed one of the most creative approaches to mysticism in modern times. What makes his approach unique is the fact that it was fostered to a remarkable degree by both his love for Earth and his devotion to science, especially the science of evolution. Teilhard's emphasis on the importance of scientific knowledge with its insistence on experience of the physical world sets his mysticism apart. Science was integral. It fueled his natural devotion and provided him with the images and a vocabulary to describe an experience that is otherwise unspeakable. Yet, despite the predominance of scientific imagery and content, Teilhard was not trying to propose a scientific theory or system. Instead, in his religious essays he was attempting to share his mystical experience so that he could "propagate . . . a certain taste, a certain perception of the beauty, the pathos, and the unity of being" (LTF, 58–59).

1

Teilhard's synthesis of religion and science has certainly been a gift to the church, even though church officials at the time were unwilling to accept his views. As a priest and scientist living and working in an era when church officials feared what seemed to them to be the theory of evolution's negative impact on Christian doctrine, Teilhard recognized instead evolution's positive potential in this regard. He was convinced that the science of evolution could help to define and energize the religion of the future. Yet this gift came with a great price. The task of integrating the theory of evolution with the doctrine of the Incarnation was not easy. It required that he passionately question both the science of his day and the religion of his heritage.

His final synthesis is the fruit of his mystical journey, a journey punctuated with both pain and ecstasy. The rejection of his synthesis by church officials who refused him permission to publish his religious essays probably was the heaviest cross that he had to bear. However, in spite of these difficulties, he never abandoned his efforts to articulate his vision, a work that he understood as a response to a call from God and a most important aspect of his religious vocation. In an endeavor to grapple with the landscapes of his mind, which were not unlike the rugged Chinese terrain that he explored during his exile, Teilhard, like Jacob wrestling with the angel, "spent his days strenuously wrestling with matter until it yielded the Divine."[1] As he hammered away at rocky terrain looking for clues about Earth's physical history and worked on his synthesis attempting to trace out Earth's spiritual history, he discovered God at Earth's very heart.

For Teilhard, mysticism is that "science of sciences which is also the supreme art and the supreme work" (MM, 268). Like most mystics, he speaks about the contemplative experience as a kind of seeing—a seeing whose fruit is the acquisition of true and complete wisdom. Mysticism is a science that

---

[1] Claude Cuénot, *Teilhard de Chardin: A Biographical Study*, trans. V. Colimore (London: Burns and Oates, 1965), 16.

requires a sixth sense, one that opens to a dimension of the world that is available to all, yet not easily accessed by many. To practice this science is to learn to discern more than that which the eye can see, the ear can hear, the nose can smell, the tongue can taste, and the skin can feel—more than what our best scientific instruments can detect. Grounded in the realities of the material world and fostered by science, Teilhard's mystical seeing requires an ability to delve beneath the surface layer of things into the reality that is embedded within. To see properly, Teilhard tells us, one must learn to notice not only the grandeur of the physical world that surrounds us but also its inner face: "Everywhere in the stuff of the Universe," he says, "there necessarily exists an internal conscious face lining the external 'material' face habitually the only one seen by science" (HP, 26). Once he was able to see this inner dimension, which he refers to as the "within" of things, Teilhard's world caught fire (HM, 15).

Seeing the inner face of the world was critical for Teilhard. In fact, he was convinced that unless the citizens of the future learn to see, humanity will perish (HP, 3). His knowledge of the dynamic processes at work in the cosmos and of the intricate structure of matter made a difference in the way he understood God's action. Contemplation of deep time and deep space highlighted for him our interdependence with one another and with our Earth. His sense of the cosmos as a single living organism led him to emphasize the global nature of the human endeavor. His awareness of humanity's impact on Earth processes affirmed the importance of human responsibility for the future. Most important, his ability to see the inner face of the world constantly allured him as he proceeded on his mystical journey. Moreover, it was his ability to see the whole of reality that he wanted so passionately to share: "It is essential to see," he says, "to see things as they are and to see them really and intensely" (D, 58), to "see God everywhere . . . in all that is most hidden, most solid, and most ultimate in the world" (D, 46). For Teilhard, the Divine Presence is "as pervasive and perceptible as the atmosphere in which we are bathed" (D, 46). Yet, despite the fact that we are encompassed on all sides by this presence, we often fail to recognize and to embrace the Divine in matter (D, 46).

Keeping one's eyes open, staying alert, and paying attention to detail are skills as important for contemplative seeing as they are for scientific investigation. In fact, for Teilhard, one mode of seeing enhances the other. For the mystic as well as for the scientist, "One must look at the thing. One must look and listen and check and question."[2] Teilhard was "convinced that there is no more substantial nourishment for religious life than contact with scientific realities, if they are properly understood" (S, 36). Thus, rather than posing a stumbling block to his spirituality, Teilhard's scientific interest and training nurtured his life of contemplation.

In an essay called "The Mystical Milieu" (W, 115–49), Teilhard provides a roadmap into the intensely mystical environment in which he lived and moved. To do this, he presents the natural roots (W, 147) and stages of his mystical growth in terms of five concentric circles. These circles, which are more properly imaged as loops of a spiral that he revisits throughout his life, provided him with steppingstones into an ever deepening reality, a reality informed as much by the science of his time as by his religious tradition. They plot his growth and development as he sinks ever more deeply into the heart of matter and into the heart of God.

His journey, he tells us, began with an awareness of a subtle Presence pervading the atmosphere in which he lived. This led him first to search for the structural consistence of the cosmos and then to investigate its inner energy. His consideration of the roots of human consciousness eventually opened him to the latent spiritual potential available within the human phenomenon and to an experience of humanity's soul. His journey culminated in the perception of the radiance

---

[2] See Marilyn Frye, "In and Out of Harm's Way: Arrogance and Love," *The Politics of Reality* (New York: Crossing Press, 1983), 66–72.

of a loving, cosmic Person—the God for evolution. Stepping with him through each of these circles, we come, gradually and logically, to understand "the substance and overflowing richness of his joy" (W, 119). We begin to see how Teilhard's mystical vision emerged, how it developed, and how we too can be drawn more and more deeply into that privileged point where the depths of our hearts and the heart of the cosmos converge with the heart of God.

My purpose here is fourfold. First of all, in language and imagery that is relevant, I trace Teilhard's journey through these circles, placing within each one events and insights from his life as a whole. I use some of his most beautiful mystical passages to tell the story of his dynamic spiritual development. Next, where appropriate, I interweave contemporary scientific examples so that the freshness of our current insights about the nature, structure, and dynamics of the cosmos will help to stimulate a sense of awe and wonder comparable to what Teilhard might have experienced when he confronted the science of his day. In recent years we have learned so much more about the cosmos in which we live: black holes are warping the fabric of spacetime; strange attractors are weaving complex patterns in response to nonlinear forces; the fundamental building blocks of nature now seem to be composed of minuscule vibrating strings; and particle interactions are being described in terms of relationship. If Teilhard were writing today, he would definitely have brought these scientific breakthroughs to bear on his mysticism. He would have wanted to learn all he could about the vastness and intricacy of the cosmos, to immerse himself in the beauty and mystery of the world that was being revealed to him, and to bring these beautiful images to his contemplation.

Since Teilhard did not limit his interests to the natural sciences, my third aim is to demonstrate how knowledge and experience of all aspects of the world—physical, social, aesthetic, and psychological—enhanced his understanding of the Divine and propelled him along his unique mystical path. Finally, I reflect on how Teilhard's unique insight into the nature and action of the Divine enabled him to visualize a world in which each person plays an integral role in the ongoing evolutionary process. His call for a global vision of humanity, a deepening consciousness, and a commitment to the evolutionary project is perhaps his most important contribution to the future of humanity.

Because the best way to understand Teilhard's mysticism is to listen to the story of his spiritual awakening as he tells it, Chapter 1 begins with a short biography presenting key moments in Teilhard's life, particularly those that shed light on his mystical journey. We are fortunate to have several of Teilhard's essays in which he relates intimate details of his life, particularly those that recount aspects of his struggle to develop and articulate his mystical vision. Chief among these sources is his autobiographical essay, "The Heart of Matter." In this essay he analyzes, with the hindsight provided by many years of reflection, the influences that effected his transformation. Written about five years before his death, this essay contains his most precious memories of a blessed, though sometimes difficult, path to integration.

In Chapters 2 through 6 we follow Teilhard as he travels ever more deeply from circle to circle into the arms of the Cosmic Christ. Along the Circle of Presence, Teilhard became attuned to the beauty of Earth, and his sensitivity to nature opened him to the Divine Presence. Images from musical acoustics, optics, and art illustrate the potential for encountering the Divine Presence in the ordinary moments of life.

In Chapter 3 we travel with Teilhard along the Circle of Consistence and explore the amazing structure of the cosmos. As we look out into the far reaches of outer space and peer down into the intimate structure of matter, we too recognize Divine Consistence that Teilhard so assiduously sought as a child.

Chapter 4 moves us on to the Circle of Energy, where, with Teilhard, we consider the process of evolution and encounter its driving force, Divine Energy. Because he focused on the overall dynamic nature of the evolutionary story rather than on the details of particular mechanisms, his portrayal of evolution continues to be relevant and inspiring. Dynamic images from star formation as well as from complexity and chaos theories enhance the scene and provide deeper insight into the mechanisms of evolution. As we explore the far reaches of outer space, peer down into the smallest-known structures of matter, and travel back through the early moments of time, we begin to sense the vastness of spacetime and the complexity of the cosmic project.

In Chapter 5 we proceed along the Circle of Spirit, where, with Teilhard, we finally break through to the inner face of evolution. There, we encounter the realm of spirit present in the noosphere, the spiritual web that forms the collective spirit of Earth. Neural network theory, a mathematical technique that attempts to mimic the complex workings of the human brain, provides a modern context in which to imagine the noosphere in its function as global brain. In the fourth circle, Teilhard's early concern about the fragility of matter and his questions about what holds matter together ultimately resolve themselves as he begins to recognize the spiritual power of matter.

Finally, in Chapter 6 we step along the Circle of Person, where, with Teilhard, we meet the person of the Cosmic Christ, the culmination of his synthesis.

Chapter 7 interprets the steps of Teilhard's journey, portrays it as a reenactment of the Incarnation, and summarizes the methods underlying Teilhard's mysticism.

As a physicist who has struggled at times to make sense of what have seemed to be the disconnected worlds of religion and science, I have relied on Teilhard to show me the way. His synthesis not only confirms that it is possible to commune deeply with both God and the world, but also teaches how to commune with God *through* the world (W, 57–59). It is my hope that this account of Teilhard's mystical experience will guide all those kindred spirits "who love the world" (D, 11) and who yearn to expand their mystical hearts.

A note on language: A number of the quotations that appear in this book were written before the current sensitivity to inclusive language was an issue. The reader is asked to read the quotations in the inclusive manner in which they were intended, even when the language used is exclusive to modern eyes.

1.

Biography

*I managed to climb up to the point where the
Universe became apparent to me
as a great rising surge,
in which all the work that goes into serious en-
quiry,
all the will to create, all the acceptance of suffering,
converge ahead into a single dazzling spear-head—
now, at the end of my life,
I can stand on the peak I have scaled and continue
to look ever more closely into the future,
and there, with ever more assurance, see the ascent
of God.*

PIERRE TEILHARD DE CHARDIN,
The Heart of Matter, 52

Pierre Teilhard de Chardin was born in 1881 in central
France near the city of Clermont-Ferrand. Having grown
up among beautiful volcanic hills as the son of an amateur
naturalist, he developed at an early age a scientist's tempera-
ment, focusing much of his attention on rock. At first, it was
not simply the beauty of the volcanic hills that fascinated
him. Rather, it was rock's relative hardness and density. This
fascination stemmed from an early experience that influenced

him profoundly, baffled him, frightened him, and seemed to arouse in him deep concern.

One day when he was about six years old, he was sitting by the fire having his hair trimmed. Suddenly, he noticed that a lock of his hair had fallen into the fire and was burning to ash. This encounter with his own mortality shocked him and caused him to search for something more permanent, more immutable, more consistent. To console himself, he began in secret to collect pieces of iron because they seemed, at first, to be the hardest of all available materials. He hid his collection in an inconspicuous part of the barn near his house and would go to visit his "god of iron" whenever he could. However, after a few rain storms and a few experiments he discovered that iron can be scratched and pitted and that, unfortunately, it eventually rusts. So, he changed his focus from iron to rock. Not realizing at the time that rock also crumbles, he sensed in rock's hardness and density something more durable than the locks of his perishable hair.

Teilhard's childhood concerns are not superficial. They initiated a lifelong research project. At an early age he had discovered and formulated both in his heart and in his head, albeit in a still very primitive way, questions that would pursue him for the rest of his life: What in the world is indestructible, permanent, enduring, eternal? And what holds the stuff of the world together? Eventually, he considered studying physics so that he could explore the theory of gravity, a topic that he thought might give him some clues about what on Earth endures and what holds everything together. The search for consistence would haunt him, motivate him, and keep him focused. It would lead him where he never expected to go and would provide him with startling new insights. His was a long and sometimes lonely, scholarly, and spiritual journey, a journey that led him into the heart of the cosmos, into the deepest part of himself, and eventually into the very heart of God.

Besides having a deep interest in science, Teilhard was also a very devout child. For this, especially for his devotion to the

Sacred Heart of Jesus, he credits his mother. As a high school student at the Jesuit-run boarding school Collège de Mongré, where he pursued his high school career, he excelled in most subjects, winning prizes in several of them even though during his classes he often preferred to think about his rocks. This was particularly true of his religion class—a class that never interested him. Nevertheless, he was attracted to the life of the Jesuits, the order who staffed the school and whose example deepened his desire to love and serve God. Soon after finishing his high school studies in 1899, he entered the novitiate of the Society of Jesus. As a young Jesuit, Teilhard was as serious about his religious life as he was about his science, and over time he continued to develop his love for and relationship with Christ.

Early in his formation period Teilhard began to wonder whether his love for rock was compatible with his love for God. He even considered abandoning his interest in geology to devote his time entirely to what he then called "supernatural" activities. Fortunately, his wise novice director encouraged him to develop both God-given gifts, and although Teilhard continued to experience and wonder at what seemed opposing tugs (HM, 46), he pursued his interest in rocks and fossils as seriously as ever. For instance, while studying philosophy on the island of Jersey off the coast of Great Britain, he took time to explore the island's geological structure, sometimes with fellow students, and with the help of Jesuit scientist Father Félix Pelletier, he eventually published a preliminary note about the island's geology and mineralogy in the Jersey Society's annual bulletin.[1]

In 1905, Teilhard was assigned to teach physics and chemistry in the Jesuit high school in Cairo, Egypt, where he also cared for the school's small museum. On free days he would take some of his students into the desert southwest of Cairo

---

[1] Claude Cuénot, *Teilhard de Chardin: A Biographical Study*, trans. V. Colimore (London: Burns and Oates, 1965), 7.

to collect all kinds of fossils, minerals, and rare insects.[2] Besides adding to the museum at the Jesuit school, he was able to send to Paris several unusual specimens collected during these expeditions.[3] In fact, the Geological Society in France named the sea fossil that he discovered during his time in Egypt *Teilhardi* in his honor.[4] By the time he left Egypt in 1908, he had already gathered enough material about the region to publish a geological and mineralogical study.[5]

In 1908, Teilhard was sent to Hastings, England, to begin his scholasticate, a time set aside during the Jesuit formation period for the study of theology. During a year of intense lecture and discussion, his scripture professors focused primarily on a verse from Saint Paul's letter to the Colossians: "In him, all things hold together" (Col 1:17b). This verse, which refers to Christ, was presented as a summation statement for all of Christology.[6] Sounding very much like the answer to his fundamental question, this passage opened Teilhard to the possibility that the integrating power of spirit might be an alternative way of viewing how things hold together, the problem of consistence. At the time, he was also reading Henri Bergson's *Creative Evolution*. When he juxtaposed the verse from Colossians against what he understood about the theory of evolution, a new insight emerged. He was suddenly able to reconcile his love for science with his love for Christ, and he developed a new understanding of the consistence of matter for which he had been searching from his boyhood (HM, 20). In what he would later call "an explosion of dazzling flashes"

---

[2] Ibid., 8.

[3] Ibid., 9.

[4] Ursula King, *Spirit of Fire: The Life and Vision of Teilhard de Chardin* (Maryknoll, NY: Orbis Books, 1996), 25. "A lepidopteron, a hymenopteron, and a fossil (a variety of Gisopygus) were named after him" (Cuénot, *Teilhard de Chardin*, 10).

[5] *The Eocene Strata of the Minieh Region*, in Cuénot, *Teilhard de Chardin*, 9.

[6] J. A. Lyons, *The Cosmic Christ in Origen and Teilhard de Chardin* (New York: Oxford University Press, 1982), 149.

(HM, 50), a unique and powerful insight was born, one that helped him visualize the unity of matter and spirit. This insight reversed his focus from the hardness of rock and the attractive power of gravity to the Spirit animating the rock and giving power to the gravitational force. He realized that "holding together" is not simply a material problem; rather, it has social and spiritual aspects as well. Through the process of evolution God is at work at the heart of matter holding all things together and drawing them into unity.

Having germinated during this period of theological study, Teilhard's ideas would continue to develop as he lived his early religious life as a scientist and would eventually form the basis for his major work, *The Human Phenomenon*. However, Teilhard would not be satisfied until his initial insight would blossom into a true synthesis of matter and spirit. It would take him years to develop fully his thought, to articulate clearly Christ's central role in the evolutionary process, and to grapple with its implications. It would become his lifelong task. But, from that moment on science and religion became inextricably so coupled for Teilhard that he would never again be able to disentangle them. Meanwhile, he continued his science walks and excursions, his search for fossils and rock, offering the specimens that he collected either to the British Museum or to the Museum at Hastings. This time, the Geological Society of London named several fossil plants, the genus *Teilhardia* and the species *Teilhardi*, in his honor.[7]

In 1911, Teilhard was ordained a priest, and in 1912, he began formal scientific study in Paris with the brilliant paleontologist and geologist Marcellin Boule, a specialist in an extinct species of pre-humans called the Neanderthals. Although he was a difficult character, Boule was quite impressed with Teilhard's gifts of penetrating observation, keenness for both minute analysis and wide synthesis, and great independence of mind.[8] Under Boule's guidance, Teilhard soon became

[7] King, *Spirit of Fire*, 40.
[8] Cuénot, *Teilhard de Chardin*, 18.

immersed in the study of the carnivore and primate fossils found in the regions in southwest France. While working on this project, Teilhard was struck by the fact that the primate group with the largest brain was the only one to survive into the present,[9] a fact that was to color his science and philosophy for years to come. This observation, relating brain size to evolutionary survival, was a piece of experimental evidence for the notion that consciousness is related to the complexity of matter and that evolution seems to be leading to ever greater consciousness. During this period Teilhard also took time to travel to northwest Spain to excavate several caverns and to admire some prehistoric cave paintings—a firsthand introduction to human prehistory.

World War I interrupted Teilhard's studies. He volunteered for military service, not as a soldier or a chaplain, but as a stretcher bearer on the front lines. The bloodshed and death that he witnessed there affected him deeply. However, during the lulls between battles, he was able to return to the ideas he had been formulating during his theological and scientific studies and began to explore them more deeply. His notebooks are full of the profound insights that resulted from his personal struggle to integrate evolution with his religious beliefs. While on the battlefront, he wrote often to his cousin Marguerite, sharing with her his initial ideas. She was the one who received the first copies of most of the essays that he wrote while in the trenches. Today, these essays can be found in a volume entitled *Writings in Time of War*. Between battles, Teilhard also engaged, as usual, in his geological interests. He took time to collect specimens, to study the geology of the trenches, and to write about the deposits he observed there.[10]

After the war Teilhard returned to his scientific studies and worked steadily on his doctoral thesis, in which he compared the mammals of the Lower Eocene period in France with those in the American Paleocene period. On March 22, 1922,

---

[9] King, *Spirit of Fire*, 42.
[10] Cuénot, *Teilhard de Chardin*, 24.

he successfully defended his thesis and began his career as a professional scientist.[11] He was appointed chair of the geology department at the Institut Catholique in Paris and lectured in geology at the École des Sciences. He developed relationships with scientists throughout the world and won several prizes.[12] His passion for synthesis was evident even in his classroom teaching. One of his students noted, for example, that after three or four hours of class, Teilhard "would have given us a unified view of the whole Carboniferous period, without our feeling at any moment that we were getting out of our depth,"[13] a real compliment for a university professor.

In 1922, Father Emile Licent, a Jesuit who had set up a small museum in Tientsin, China, urged Teilhard to join him to assist with the classification of the remains of some fossil mammals that he had found on recent expeditions in China.[14] Teilhard had already been advising Licent about samples sent to the Paris Museum. By May 1923, Teilhard found himself in China, living and working with Licent. Their first expedition was to the Ordos Desert, a vast plateau in western Mongolia enclosed by the Yellow River. Because the presence of bandits and lack of water made it dangerous to go directly, they decided to take a roundabout route. They began their dig on the banks of the Shara-Osso-Gol, a strange little river that runs at the bottom of a canyon, where they found many fossils and prehistoric implements. They also discovered traces of Paleolithic man and gathered many perfectly preserved animal fossils as well as about one-half a ton of several-hundred-thousand-year-old worked stones that had probably been used

---

[11] Ibid., 30.

[12] He worked with Stehlin from Basle, Plymen from England, Wong from China, and Granger from America. He was also awarded several prizes for his scientific work—in 1922, the Prix Viquesnel given by the Société Géologique de France; in 1923, the Prix Roux given by the Académie des Sciences; and in 1924, he was elected member of the Société de biogéographie (Ibid., 31–32).

[13] Ibid., 33.

[14] Ibid., 43.

as tools and weapons. These were eventually sent to France. It was during this expedition that Teilhard finished writing "The Mass on the World," an intensely moving articulation of his eucharistic spirituality that he had begun in the Aisne forest during World War I. In it he portrays the Cosmic Christ, incarnate at the heart of matter, transforming the whole Earth with our active participation.[15]

Teilhard decided to stay in China through the spring of 1924, sorting the specimens that he and Licent had found, writing up his notes, attending a meeting of geologists, visiting other scientists in Peking, making shorter expeditions to the south of Peking, and finally setting out to explore the region to the north.[16]

On his return to Paris, Teilhard took up his former position at the Institut Catholique, worked at the Paris Museum, and reconnected with friends and scholars. He continued to focus on the mammals of the Tertiary and Quaternary periods, especially fossil rodents, and was becoming known as a specialist in this field. He was also quickly gaining in popularity with college students and seminarians because of the freshness and creativity of his vision, and he was often invited to speak on evolution.[17] This provided him with a chance to share his continually refined synthesis. However, this state of affairs did not last long. It soon became clear to church authorities, who were still suspicious of the theory of evolution and its potentially negative impact on church doctrine, that Teilhard's views, particularly those relating to original sin, were contrary to their own.

In 1926, Teilhard wrote a personal note for a colleague interested in his views on the topic of original sin. This note mysteriously disappeared from Teilhard's desk drawer and arrived on the desk of church officials in Rome. Because the views put forth in this note seemed to clash with church

---

[15] King, *Spirit of Fire*, 100–101.
[16] Cuénot, *Teilhard de Chardin*, 51.
[17] Ibid., 59–60.

doctrine, Teilhard was forbidden by his religious superiors to lecture on these topics, ordered to confine himself to purely scientific lectures and publications, required to sign an agreement never to speak or write about these ideas, and told to leave Paris. His superiors assumed that, with Teilhard away from the spotlight, the interest in evolution that he was generating would settle down. Deeply distressed, Teilhard finally, though reluctantly, submitted to this request and signed the agreement. By the end of April he was back in China establishing his home in Tientsin with Licent. On his way back to China he received word that his connection with the Institut Catholique had been permanently severed.[18] Although he was still permitted to return to Paris periodically for visits and to stay connected to his circle of scientific contacts, he was never again to teach there or to exert the kind of influence he once had there.

In China, Teilhard resumed his expeditions, traveling ever further into the regions that surround Peking. Licent, who had established a museum in Tientsin, was primarily a collector with little talent for classification, generalization, and synthesis. These were instead Teilhard's great gifts. Licent preferred to work alone, while Teilhard was eager to collaborate, especially with the Chinese scientists. The fact that they did not see eye to eye made life difficult for both Teilhard and Licent. Yet, somehow they managed to work out their differences. Little by little, though, Teilhard spent more time in Peking, where he enjoyed the cosmopolitan atmosphere and was stimulated by the scientific research activity that occurred there as well as by the many chances for collaboration. By 1931, Peking became his official residence.[19]

Teilhard was involved with many excavations. The site of the most illustrious of these is located at Zhóu-Kóu-Tien, thirty miles southwest of Peking—about a day's mule ride. There, Teilhard eventually helped to locate a cave that contained

---

[18] Ibid., 63.
[19] King, *Spirit of Fire*, 126.

pre-human fossils. In 1926, two pre-human teeth were found; by 1928, two fragments of a jawbone; by the end of 1929, an uncrushed adult skull; eventually, skull caps, skeletal bones, and teeth from about fourteen individuals as well as several hundred pounds of artifacts.[20] The newly discovered species, called Sinanthropus or Peking man, lived about 500,000 years ago and used stone tools and perhaps fire. Teilhard was chief geologist at the site, and although not directly responsible for this find, he made many valuable contributions to the project. For instance, as a skilled stratigrapher, he analyzed the layers of sedimentary rock and realized that the area where this significant find took place was actually an enormous filled-in cavern.[21]

In 1931, Teilhard was appointed as a scientist to accompany the Croisière Jaune or Yellow Crossing, a nine-month automobile expedition into the interior of China organized by the Citroën automobile company of France.[22] It was a rugged and somewhat disappointing trip for Teilhard in many ways, but he made the best of it—working tirelessly along the way, learning much about the geology of the far west of China, and integrating what he saw into what he already knew about the geology of China. During the years that followed the Croisière Jaune, Teilhard spent most of his time working in Peking at the Chinese Geological Survey and at Zhóu-Kóu-Tien. He contributed to the field of paleontology in China by encouraging and solidly educating the young Chinese scientists, attending international conferences, writing papers for the *Geological Review*, updating his scientific memoirs, and continuing his expeditions throughout China. Teilhard also traveled to India, Pakistan, Burma, and Java, doing field work and visiting geological sites such as the location where the fossils of Java man had been found. In his spare time he continued developing his ideas in a raft of religious essays.

---

[20] Ibid., 130.
[21] Cuénot, *Teilhard de Chardin*, 98.
[22] Ibid., 125.

Despite the fact that his religious superiors frustrated all efforts to publish his religious writings, he never stopped trying to articulate his vision or to share his ideas with friends. By 1939, the political climate in Peking had become very difficult. Japan occupied the city while war was raging in other parts of China. During the war years Teilhard's activity, particularly his travel, was curtailed; field work was next to impossible; many of his friends had already left China; communication with the outside world was poor. Concerned for the precious fossils and artifacts, particularly those that had been found at Zhóu-Kóu-Tien, the French government offered space for the lab at a site near the French Embassy in Peking. After moving the valuable specimens Teilhard and his friend Jesuit Pierre Leroy established the Peking Institute of Geobiology at the new site, hoping that it would one day become a continental research center.[23] Because of the political turmoil of the time, many scientists moved to the south of China so that they would be able to continue their work. Teilhard, however, refused to follow, staying instead in Peking to guard the valuable specimens. He worked each day at the Peking Union Medical College with the Zhóu-Kóu-Tien fossils, but he was no longer able to do field work. He missed field work terribly, but the leisure this void created provided him time to work on his most important treatise, *The Human Phenomenon*, which was not published until after his death in 1955. In spite of his care for the Sinanthropus fossils, they were eventually lost. Though never confirmed, it is presumed that they were sent to the United States with American soldiers and were probably in Pearl Harbor when the Japanese bombed the city. By 1946, Teilhard finally had returned to Paris. Unfortunately, he left behind his many books, papers, and diaries, and they too have been lost.

While in Paris, Teilhard spent time recuperating from a heart attack and several bouts of nervous depression. His physical illness was at least in part due to the conflict he was

---

[23] King, *Spirit of Fire*, 178.

experiencing with his Jesuit and church superiors regarding the publication of *The Human Phenomenon*. In the end they denied his request to publish and advised him to leave Paris. Now seventy years old, he took up residence in New York City. On the way to New York, he participated in his last geological expeditions. In South Africa he viewed, among other things, the remains of Australopithecus. Then he traveled on to Buenos Aires, Rio de Janeiro, and Trinidad, always interested in the geological structures that he encountered, always revising his theories of the dynamic story of Earth's global geology. In New York City he served as research associate at the Wenner Gren Foundation, a foundation heavily involved in anthropological research. Teilhard worked there until his sudden death on Easter Day, April 10, 1955.

On June 25, 1947, the French Foreign Affairs Ministry promoted Teilhard to the rank of officer of the Legion of Honor with the following citation:

> For outstanding services to the intellectual and scientific influence of France, through a body of work mostly written and published in China, which has established him as a leading authority in international, and particularly in English-speaking, scientific circles. He may now be regarded, in the field of paleontology and geology, as one of the chief ornaments of French science, whose international standing he has done much, by his personal contacts with foreign scientists, to maintain and exalt.[24]

This is a fitting tribute to one so dedicated to the furthering of scientific research. Widely respected in the international scientific community and in communication with the top scientists in his field, Teilhard created a vast body of scientific scholarship. Sadly, it was not until after his death in 1955,

---

[24] Jeanne Mortier and Marie-Louise Aboux, eds., *Teilhard de Chardin Album* (New York: Harper and Row, 1966), 176.

when his religious writing began to be published,[25] that he would be held in esteem by people throughout the world who share his religious questions and who, like him, are searching for a way to understand their faith in the light of scientific discoveries. Thankfully, Teilhard never gave up, even in the face of strong opposition. Today, we reap the fruits of his marvelous integration of faith and science, a mystical vision that supported him throughout his life and made it possible for him to persevere to the end.

---

[25] Since his death Teilhard's religious writings have been published in thirteen volumes; his scientific works, many of which are published in scientific journals, have been collected in eleven volumes.

2.

The Circle of Presence

There were moments, indeed, when it seemed to me that a sort of universal being was about to take shape suddenly in Nature before my very eyes.

PIERRE TEILHARD DE CHARDIN,
The Heart of Matter, 26

Teilhard's mystical journey began in the Circle of Presence. A nature lover from his youth, he was strongly affected by the lush beauty of the sense world that surrounded him. Something as simple as a song, a sunbeam, a fragrance, or a glance would pierce his heart and heighten his awareness of an unexplainable presence. The aesthetic pleasure that these encounters elicited enveloped him and penetrated to the depths of his soul. Although such moments were fleeting, they set up cosmic vibrations that invaded his being and took possession of him. Such encounters opened him to a new dimension that he yearned to explore. They stirred in him a desire to become one with the cosmos, to become "immersed in an Ocean of matter" (HM, 20). Each encounter fostered in him "an insatiable desire to maintain contact . . . with a sort of universal root of being" (HM, 20). Apparent from his childhood, Teilhard's openness to this numinous presence would continue to grow within him in clarity and in depth. This innate ability to lose himself in the numinous would lead him to experience a Divine Presence gleaming at the heart of matter.

Many people are surprised that Teilhard, a scientist who understood so well the physical properties of sound and light, would give himself over to the lure that these moments can provide. Yet, the pleasure that came to him from contact with the physical world stimulated his mystical life and provided him with images capable of describing an experience that is otherwise unutterable. Moreover, his strong understanding of physical phenomena served to further amplify his mystical sense.

Teilhard's love affair with rock, his captivation with its hardness and density, and his overwhelming natural appetite for the solid, the everlasting, and the changeless initiated him into the world of mysticism. So profound was his passion for rock that he eventually chose geology and paleontology as fields of graduate study, fields for which he showed great natural talent. Throughout his life he was ever on the lookout for fossils and unusual specimens of rock, "never without his geologist's hammer, his magnifying glass, and his notebook." Years of careful collecting found him "gifted with very sharp sight." In fact, his friends claim that "his quick eye would catch any chipped or chiselled stone that lay on the ground."[1] This sensitivity to the shape of the arrowhead and the print of the fossil kept him always alert to the beauty and texture of the landscape.[2]

---

[1] Claude Cuénot, *Teilhard de Chardin: A Biographical Study*, trans. V. Colimore (London: Burns and Oates, 1965), 129, 156, 91.

[2] According to those who knew him, Teilhard had a marvelous talent for observation. "George Le Febre, for example, noted . . . that 'his downcast eyes would spot the smallest bit of cut stone betraying itself by its redness on the bare greyness of the wind-swept soil'" (Cuénot, *Teilhard de Chardin*, 91). His co-worker George Barbour notes that he "could spot a single Palaeolithic implement in a bed of gravel three metres away without dismounting" (ibid., 156). His friend Helmut de Terra says that he "recognized Palaeolithic artifacts with an uncanny sort of instinct. Often he would pick one of these from the ground, look at it

Field work in geology and paleontology brought Teilhard great satisfaction. His professional activity entailed observing geological formations and searching for fossils and primitive tools to discover clues about how Earth's rocky surface evolved and how the variety of life forms emerged on Earth. These pursuits satisfied his need for prolonged contact with Earth. They were his way of touching what he sensed was animating and directing everything (LT, 66). The sparks of Divine Presence that he discerned within Earth's rocky layers enlivened him, nourished him,[3] and fueled his desire to be fused with Earth. They helped him to deepen his relationship with a Presence, "a sort of universal root or matrix of beings" (HM, 20).

Although Teilhard focused much of his attention on rock, he was actually a keen observer of the natural world in whatever form it presented itself and never missed a chance to enjoy Earth's beauty. Letters to friends and family are full of observations about the people that he met, the work that he was doing, and the thoughts that he was thinking. But they are also full of rich and sensuous detail about the landscape. For instance, he wrote to his cousin Marguerite that "cranes, swans, geese, spoonbills and beautiful ducks with dazzling plumage nest and swim almost as fearlessly as the birds in a public garden" (LT, 119). During his long ocean voyages he often spent time contemplating the beauty of the sea and sky. In a letter to Marguerite written on his way to China, he described an unusual sunset:

> Yesterday I could never tire of looking to the east where the sea was uniformly milky and green, with an opalescence that was still not transparent, lighter than the background of the sky. Suddenly on the horizon a thin diffuse cloud became tinged with pink; and then with

---

briefly from all sides, and hand it to me, saying: 'It is suspicious; we must find more to be absolutely sure'" (ibid., 190).

[3] Ibid., 33n27.

the little oily ripples of the ocean still open on one side
and turning to lilac on the other, the whole sea looked
for a few seconds like watered silk. Then the light was
gone and the stars began to be reflected around us as
peacefully as in the water of a quiet pool. (LT, 67)

The songs of the birds and their plumage, the wild hum of
insects, the tireless blooming of the flowers (W, 194)—all of
these touched him deeply. His senses were alive to the colors,
odors, and sounds that enveloped him. In one of his wartime
essays, he remarked: "I have contemplated nature for so long
and have so loved her countenance" (W, 32).

Teilhard often found himself drawn by something shining
at the heart of matter (HM, 17). Nature exerted power over
him. A mysterious inner clarity seemed to transfigure for him
every being and event (HM, 15). In an early essay he wrote:
"I have always loved and sought to read the face of Nature;
but . . . my approach has not been that of the 'scientist' but
that of the votary" (HM, 198). Reverence, awe, and devotion
were aspects of this exquisite relationship. Later in life, while
reflecting on the days when he studied theology in Hastings,
he still vividly recalled

the extraordinary solidity and intensity I found then in
the English countryside, particularly at sunset, when
the Sussex woods were charged with all that "fossil"
Life which I was then hunting for, from cliff to quarry.
. . . There were moments, indeed, when it seemed to me
that a sort of universal being was about to take shape
suddenly in Nature before my very eyes. (HM, 25–26)

The aesthetic aspect of his encounter with nature served to
amplify the pleasure he derived from the experience. As he
gave himself over to nature's allure, Beauty reverberated at
the very core of his being (W, 117) and drew him out of himself, filling him with "an impassioned awareness of a wider
expansion and an all-embracing unity" (W, 118). In fact, he

claimed that he was "so surrounded and transfixed by [the Divine Presence], that there was no room left to fall down and adore" (D, 112).

Teilhard's senses were particularly alert to the interaction of sunlight with the landscape. Like Impressionist artist Claude Monet, who tried to capture in his paintings the play of sunlight on water, haystacks, and water lilies as it changed throughout the day, Teilhard was fascinated with the way the sun's "deep brilliance" (D, 130) seemed to make "the whole surface of things sparkle" (LTF, 123). For instance, he described the view from the window of the room that he occupied in Tientsin, China: "I still have a wide vista of fields and fresh water which enchants me every evening with the sweetness and purity of the hues it takes on in the setting sun" (LTF, 50). In his letters he would often mention unusually beautiful details about his surroundings, such as the "large black butterflies with metallic-green reflections and long tails" (LTF, 39), or the way "the sea often becomes sleek and oily . . . its surface . . . white and opaque, like milk," or how storms that break over the mountains "form thick clouds which the setting sun paints glorious colors" (LTF, 24). He was always conscious of the landscape.

Teilhard's sensitivity to light and color opened another pathway to the Divine Presence. It began, he says, "with a diffused radiance which haloed every beauty" that day by day became "more fragrant, more coloured, more intense" (D, 129). Sometimes, he was enchanted with "the play of colours on a transparent bubble" (HU, 44); at other times, a crown of light seemed to surround everything and disclose the unique essence of the universe (W, 119). Just as rays of sunlight strike dust particles, making the rays suddenly visible to the eye, so Divine Light impinged on his inner eyes from all sides and caressed them (W, 118). And like the reflections caused by "sunlight in the fragments of a broken mirror" (D, 114), this Light was reflected and scattered in all directions so that his inner world eventually became luminous (W, 246). Speaking of the Divine Light, he said: "This light is not the superficial glimmer . . . nor is it the violent flash which destroys objects and blinds our eyes. It is the calm and powerful radiance engendered by the synthesis of all the elements of the world" (D, 130).

Teilhard compared the Divine Presence that he experienced "gleaming at the heart of matter" (J, 13) with a candle that is placed within a lamp constructed from translucent materials. When candlelight penetrates the outer covering of such a lamp, it transfigures the lamp from within. For Teilhard, nature, like the lamp, is continually "bathed in an inward light" (D, 130).

Not only could Teilhard see the light of Divine Presence, but he could also taste it. It not only filled his eyes but also impregnated his affections and thoughts (W, 118). As his perception of the inner light intensified and its color became more brilliant, he was drawn to explore its nature and to bathe in its warmth. This inner light, he says, "becomes perceptible and attainable . . . in the crystalline transparency of beings" (D, 73). He wanted only this light: "If the light is extinguished, because the object is out of place, or has outlived its function, or has moved itself, then even the most precious substance is only ashes" (D, 73).

Although he was able to write essays with a poetic flair, Teilhard sometimes wished that he had been gifted with a talent for music instead. Because music is more immediate than language, it "has a much larger world of associations at its disposal"[4] and speaks more directly to the soul.[5] Its ambivalent and ephemeral nature and the intangibility of its content would have afforded him, he thought, a better means of communicating his mystical experience to others. To one of

---

[4] Daniel Barenboim, *Music Quickens Time* (Brooklyn, NY: Verso, 2008), 3.

[5] For a discussion of Teilhard and music, see Thomas M. King, SJ, "Teilhard, Beauty, and the Arts," in *Rediscovering Teilhard's Fire*, ed. Kathleen Duffy, SSJ (Philadelphia: St. Joseph's University Press, 2010).

his friends he confided: "I would like to . . . translate as faith-
fully as possible what I hear murmuring in me like a voice or
a song which are not of me, but of the World in me" (LTF,
44). Yet, in his efforts to express his mystical experience, he
found that "it is not possible to transmit directly by words
the perception of a quality, a taste" (LTF, 59).

He noted how certain types of sound, and particularly
music, poetry, and uplifting conversation, feed the soul: "If
even the most humble and most material of our foods is
capable of deeply influencing our most spiritual faculties,
what can be said of the infinitely more penetrating energies
conveyed to us by the music of tones, of notes, of words, of
ideas?" (D, 59). Although the stimulus of color provided him
much nourishment, it was more often "the magic of sound
passing through my ears as a vibration and emerging in my
brain in the form of an inspiration" (HP, 29) that moved
him. He realized that music can excite powerful emotions—
sometimes simply by allowing a single musical tone to arise
from the silence, or, at other times, by weaving into an intricate harmony several voices, each with its own melodic
beauty.[6] In fact, composers have at their disposal a glorious
diversity of melodies, harmonies, tempos, intensities, and
rhythms that can effectively excite emotional response:[7]
the sound of a cello or of a French horn playing a haunt-
ing melody, the interplay of voices in a fugue, the complex
rhythms of jazz—each of these can cause delight at a level
beyond the auditory and can open the listener to love. By
first setting a mood of anticipation and then by providing
either immediate satisfaction or postponed gratification with
the use of carefully controlled dissonances, musicians engage
the listener at a deep level.

---

[6] Leonard Bernstein, *The Joy of Music* (New York: Simon and
Schuster, 1959), 239.

[7] Robert Jourdain, *Music, the Brain, and Ecstasy: How Music Captures Our Imagination* (New York: William Morrow, 1997), 309, 312.

"Hearing is a way of touching at a distance."[8] To the complex organ that is the human ear and to the brain that eventually relays its message to the rest of the body, this touch can be gentle and loving or harsh and cold. Molecules of air are collected by the shell-shaped pinna of the outer ear and then pound against the eardrum causing it to vibrate. These vibrations set up mechanical waves in the middle ear that are next transformed into pressure waves in the inner ear and finally into the electrical signals that are transmitted to the brain. This complex aural mechanism allows us to differentiate tones and to appreciate harmonies. Although we are often unaware of the soundscape in which we are embedded and of its effect on our psyches, our ears are constantly bombarded with sound waves—nature sounds such as the howl of a strong, gusty wind, the song of a bird, mechanical sounds from traffic and motors, and background music. And when we do become aware, it is difficult to close off our ears to unwanted sonic incursions. Our outer ears are at the mercy of whatever noise pollution is being broadcast through the air at any moment. "Music," on the other hand, "educates our ears making us more receptive and sensitive to our sound environment."[9]

From his study of physics Teilhard would have had a rich understanding of the physical basis for harmony. He would have known how the human ear is trained and how the mind is psychologically conditioned to respond favorably to certain harmonies, to certain combinations of tones that work well together. Although composers have intuited how to assemble consonant combinations and have constructed rules to guide harmonic practice, scientists have been able to demonstrate

---

[8] R. Murray Schafer, *The Tuning of the World: A Pioneering Exploration into the Past History and Present State of the Most Neglected Aspect of Our Environment: The Soundscape* (New York: Alfred A. Knopf, 1977), 11.

[9] John M. Ortiz, *The Tao of Music: Sound Psychology—Using Music to Change Your Life* (York Beach, ME: Samuel Weiser, 1997), 213.

a physical basis for their choices. Structures in the cochlea of the inner ear determine the kinds of harmonies that are pleasing. Auditory signals that enter the cochlea cause hairs along the basilar membrane to vibrate in resonance at the same frequency, causing some combinations to be pleasing and others to be disturbing. Tones that are very close in frequency excite hairs that are quite close together along the basilar membrane, thus producing a physical disturbance in the ears that renders the combination dissonant.

For centuries, the frequencies and intensities of the overtones produced by pipe and string have served as the basis for the harmonic practice of Western music. Pipes and strings produce harmonic overtones, patterns of consonant sounds that blend well together. Yet, harmonic practice differs from culture to culture and from age to age, and as composers continue to experiment with new combinations of sound, new rules emerge. In recent years composers have experimented with a variety of musical harmonies, including those that avoid a tonal center and those with musical tones whose frequencies fit somewhere between two of the adjacent tones that make up the chromatic scale.

Even though Teilhard was not able to compose music, he often used the language of musical acoustics to describe his experience of Presence. By doing so, he hoped to show others how to listen to their inner music and become caught up in its charm. The resonant frequencies of a plucked string or of an open or closed pipe had their counterpart in the resonant response of his heart to the inner music that delighted him. The harmonious sound created by the interplay of seemingly divergent voices spoke to him of the great harmony of communion that is the goal of all mystical experience and the direction toward which it points.

The music of Teilhard's outer world initiated the music of his inner world. "It began," he says, "with a particular and unique resonance which swelled each harmony" (D, 129). His initial sensitivity to nature sounds helped him to listen more deeply for that unique musical tone that was singing in his heart. Just as

> all the sounds of created being are fused, without being confused, in a single note which dominates and sustains them . . . so all the powers of the soul begin to resound in response to its call; and these multiple tones, in their turn, compose themselves into a single, ineffably simple vibration in which all the spiritual nuances—of love and of ecstasy, of passion and of indifference, of assimilation and of surrender, of rest and of motion—are born and pass and shine forth. (D, 120)

Not only did Teilhard experience the Divine Presence radiating from within all things, but he also heard this Presence pulsating at the heart of matter (HE, 123). "There is a . . . note," he says, "which makes the whole World vibrate" (LTF, 31) with "a vibration that passes all description, inexhaustible in the richness of its tones and its notes, interminable in the perfection of its unity" (S, 39). The "resonance that lies muted in the depth of every human" (W, 101) caused the very core of his being to vibrate in response (HU, 46). Like a musical instrument, his spirit resonated with the unique tone emitted by the Divine Presence, and within his whole being, he felt reverberate "an echo as vast as the universe" (W, 101).

For Teilhard, the duty of the mystic is to be aware of the inner rhythm of the world and to listen with care for the heartbeat of a higher reality (W, 119). As a result of this kind of listening, he was drawn out of himself "into a wider harmony . . . into an ever richer and more spiritual rhythm" (W, 117), so that he eventually became "caught up in the essential music of the world" (W, 101) and responded to "the fundamental harmony of the Universe" (LTF, 59). At this privileged place, he tells us, "the least of our desires and efforts . . . can . . . cause the marrow of the universe to vibrate" (D, 115). "Indeed," he wrote, "we are called by the music of the universe to reply, each with his own pure and incommunicable harmonic" (HE, 150).

In music as in life, listening to the other, entering into the emotions of the other is as important as expressing oneself. Performers must be aware of the relationship between their own voice and the many other voices with which they are conversing. Beauty and balance are achieved only when each strand of a polyphonic texture is played so distinctly and woven together so smoothly that each voice can be heard and appreciated as part of a single whole.[10] Teilhard's sensitivity to music and to nature sounds kept him ever attentive to the Divine, whose heartbeat reverberates within each and every fragment of the world (C, 63) and whose voice becomes evident to those who know how to hear. It was this voice that guided him as he encountered and responded to the joys and sufferings that composed his life.

Yet, despite his extreme sensitivity to the music of the cosmos, Teilhard sometimes felt like "a deaf man straining in his effort to hear a music which he knows to be all around him" (LTF, 40). The Divine Presence is elusive. Just as the penetrating energies of a musical experience delight the heart and elicit a subtle response only to fade into silence, a mystical experience often lasts but a moment and then evaporates with only its memory to haunt us.[11] However, especially toward the end of his life, Teilhard found himself constantly aware of the Divine Presence.

Unlike the sense of hearing, the sense of smell is a direct sense and one that often arouses vivid memories. Organic molecules called esters evaporate from a fragrant substance, float through the air, enter the nostrils, travel to the top of the nasal passages past the hair-like projections called cilia that filter out dirt from the air, dissolve in the mucous, and bond to the smell receptors located on the olfactory receptor neurons in the nasal epithelium. This bonding triggers neurons

---

[10] Barenboim, *Music Quickens Time*, 53, 50, 131.
[11] Ibid., 7.

in the brain, which then interprets and classifies the stimulant as one of about ten thousand potential odors, and causes the perception of smell.

Just as he was so deeply moved by Earth's sights and sounds, Teilhard was also alive to Earth's fragrance, to the "atmosphere heavy with the smell of orange trees in bloom," to the "hot desert regions of Arabia, all perfumed with incense and coffee" (LTF, 24), to the flowers such as the lilac and lavender that "smelt good and sparkled gaily in the hot light" (LT, 97). These lovely scents allured him and encouraged him to "hasten . . . freely and passionately" (W, 192) along the mystical path.

Teilhard also came to recognize and to respond to the Divine Presence shining through the eyes of others. While pursuing his doctorate in geology and paleontology in Paris at the Institut Catholique, the Collège de France, and the Musée d'Histoire Naturelle, he spent time with his cousin Marguerite Teillard-Chambon, whom he had not seen since they were young children. The two found that they had similar interests and developed at that time a deep and lasting relationship. As they shared what was deepest in their souls, Teilhard was drawn to the light he saw shining from Marguerite's face. "A light glows for a moment in the depths of the eyes I love. . . . And, under the glance that fell upon me, the shell in which my heart slumbered, burst open" (W, 117–18). A new energy emerged from within, causing him to feel as vast and as rich as the universe. Marguerite had awakened the feminine aspect of his being. His love for her drew him out of himself, sensitized him, and stimulated his capacity for deeper and more intimate relationships.[12]

As a stretcher bearer during the war, Teilhard had occasion to look into the eyes of many a dying soldier. Just before the moment of death, a strange light would often appear in

---

[12] See Ursula King, *Spirit of Fire: The Life and Vision of Teilhard de Chardin* (Maryknoll, NY: Orbis Books, 1996), 75.

a soldier's eyes. Teilhard was never sure whether the eyes were filled with "unspeakable agony or . . . with an excess of triumphant joy" (HM, 65). Each time the light went out and the wounded soldier died, Teilhard was overcome with a deep sense of sadness. Goethe once wrote that "every new object, well contemplated, opens up a new organ of perception in us."[13] This assertion certainly proved true for Teilhard. Overwhelmed by nature's grandeur, he seemed capable of perceiving ever new dimensions within the texture of the cosmos.

> This scintillation of beauties was so total, so all embracing, and at the same time so swift, that it reached down into the very powerhouse of my being, flooding through it in one surge, so that my whole self vibrated to the very core . . . with a full note of explosive bliss that was completely and utterly unique. (HM, 65).

In response to the diverse and captivating beauties that surrounded him, "all the elements of his psychological life were in turn affected; sensations, feelings, thoughts" (D, 129). He was experiencing an emotion that

> is impossible (once one has experienced it) to confuse with any other spiritual emotion, whether joy in knowledge or discovery, joy in creation or in loving: and this not so much because it is different from all those emotions, but because it belongs to a higher order and contains them all. (HM, 17)

Contact with the beauty of nature and of person began to break down the sense of radical separation that he would naturally experience between himself and others, between

---

[13] Johann Wolfgang von Goethe, *Goethe's Werke: Hamburger Ausgabe*, vol. 13, 5th ed. (Hamburg: Christian Wegner, 1966), 51.

subject and object,[14] and began the process of dissolving his dependency on his ego. The more deeply touched he was by Beauty in whatever form—whether a soft touch, a brilliant tone, an exquisite flavor, or a delicate tint—the more he felt free to experience true union with the other (W, 117–18). Beauty "drew me out of myself, into a wider harmony than that which delights the senses, into an ever richer and more spiritual rhythm" (W, 117). Being captured by something outside himself and losing himself in something beyond himself was an effective step toward disempowering his ego.[15] Moments of ecstasy blurred the boundaries of his being, engulfed him in feelings that were oceanic, and revealed his bonds to the larger world.[16] He began to see with the eyes of an artist who is sensitive to the soul's inner currents (LTF, 30), so that Beauty found its way into his life and healed his wounds.[17] These ecstatic moments gave him a greater grasp of the world,[18] enabling him to move away from feelings of isolation and to perceive the "unity of a higher order" (W, 15). As a result, he became capable of stepping forth from his self-imposed and imagined limits, of surrendering his autonomy, and of opening himself to the larger reality that was presenting itself to him.[19] Having invaded his being and penetrated to its core, having pierced through to its depths, Beauty drew him into that single privileged point where Divine Presence exists equally everywhere, and where all diversities and all impurities yearn to melt away.

Although Teilhard was overcome by the sensible beauty of nature, he eventually realized that to become absorbed in what is beautiful is not satisfying enough. Somehow, he knew

---

[14] See Thomas M. King, *Teilhard's Mysticism of Knowing* (New York: Seabury Press, 1981), 67.

[15] Dorothee Soelle, *The Silent Cry: Mysticism and Resistance* (Minneapolis: Fortress Press, 2001), 212.

[16] Jourdain, *Music, the Brain, and Ecstasy*, 327.

[17] Soelle, *The Silent Cry*, 222.

[18] Jourdain, *Music, the Brain, and Ecstasy*, 331.

[19] Soelle, *The Silent Cry*, 27.

that matter itself was not the true source of his joy. Instead, he was actually being allured by the Divine Presence embedded deep within the sensible world, drawn inward ultimately to be invited to flow outward (W, 118). Rather than holding him prisoner, Beauty continually reawakened him to an impassioned awareness of a wider expansion and an all-embracing unity. Once having entered into the very depths of his being, Beauty would withdraw from him and bear him away.

Earth's beauty fed Teilhard's soul and led him to perceive something shining at the heart of matter. Illuminated by the radiance that emerges from its very Center, the world became transparent. He savored this experience. He "had in fact acquired a new sense, *the sense of a new quality . . . of a new dimension*. Deeper still: a transformation had taken place . . . *in the very perception of being*" (D, 129). He had reached a place "in which things, while retaining their habitual texture, seem to be made out of a different substance" (W, 246), a place where the Divine Presence "*discloses itself to us as a modification of the deep being of things*" (D, 130). Teilhard was learning something that Thomas Merton expresses so well:

> There is in all visible things an invisible fecundity, a dimmed light, a meek namelessness, a hidden wholeness.
> . . . There is in all things an inexhaustible sweetness and purity, a silence that is a fount of action and joy. It rises up in wordless gentleness and flows out . . . from the unseen roots of all created being, welcoming me tenderly, saluting me with indescribable humility.[20]

Teilhard knew the Divine Presence as "a seeing, a taste . . . a sort of intuition bearing upon certain superior qualities in things." This experience "cannot be attained directly by any process of reasoning, nor by any human artifice" (D, 131). He

---

[20] Christopher Pramuk, *Sophia: The Hidden Christ of Thomas Merton* (Collegeville, MN: Liturgical Press, 2009), 301.

knew that underlying Earth's surface charms a vivid Presence lies hidden within and penetrates all things. This was the only source that could give him light and the only air that he could ever breathe (W, 123). He yearned to sharpen his sensibilities so that he could see ever more deeply into the heart of matter. Along the first circle, the palpable world had truly become for him a holy place (D, 112), a divine milieu, permeated with a vast, formidable, and charming presence. Clearly, this was "a gift, like life itself" (D, 131), a gift for which he was most grateful.

3.

The Circle of Consistence

Everywhere there are traces of, and a yearning for,
a unique support, a unique and absolute soul,
a unique reality in which other realities are brought
together in synthesis,
as stable and universal as matter, as simple as
spirit.

—-Pierre Teilhard de Chardin,
Writings in Time of War, 124

Teilhard's awareness of the vibrant Presence, reflected from matter and refracted through the crystalline transparency of things, lured him further along his mystical path and deeper into the cosmos. As he moved beyond the Circle of Presence and stepped onto the Circle of Consistence, his ability to see and to be drawn by matter expanded. In this new phase of his life he focused not only on the beauty of nature but also on the properties and structure of the cosmos as a whole. Although his perception of its outer features and its inner light was already quite keen, in the Circle of Consistence new qualities emerged that had so far eluded him.

Teilhard's awakening to the cosmos was the result of his love affair with what he considered at the time to be the most tangible and concrete form of matter—rock (HM, 17–21).

As a child he had been concerned about matter's transient nature and was attracted to anything that was hard, heavy, tough, and durable (HM, 18). In fact, he began his mystical journey worshiping first iron, and then bits of quartz and amethyst crystals, especially those "glittering fragments of chalcedony" (HM, 19). Disturbed by the fragility of other forms of matter, he found the mineral world hard, resistant, impervious to attack (HM, 19), and thus worthy of adoration. His choice to abandon his collection of iron scraps for rock was fortunate since it led him from mere rock collecting to the study of Earth's crust and eventually expanded his thinking to the planetary scale. Later in life, he noted how fortunate this choice was. "It was precisely through the gateway that the substitution of Quartz for Iron opened for my groping mind into the vast structures of the Planet and of Nature, that I began, without realizing it, truly to make my way into the World—until nothing could satisfy me that was not on the scale of the universal" (HM, 19). Having begun his exploration among the beautiful hills of the Auvergne, his interest in the science of geology clearly thrust him into the very depths and breadth of the cosmos.

As a professional researcher, Teilhard was averse to simply collecting and cataloguing specimens. Instead, he preferred to think on a continental scale, to determine the inner and outer structures of matter, and to discover what holds matter together. He was ever on the lookout for "an ultimate Element in which all things find their definitive consistence" (W, 123). Field work in geology and paleontology put him in touch with Earth at its most intimate level; travel throughout Asia—especially China—Africa, and North America encouraged a global perspective. But it was his brief study of physics that initiated his interest in the cosmos as a whole. Electrons, nuclei, waves, and the force of gravity stirred his imagination (HM, 23). At first, it seemed as if the theory of gravity might contain the answer to his fundamental question, "What holds everything together?" In fact, at age twenty-two, he was so convinced of this that he decided to dedicate himself one day to unlocking gravity's secrets (HM, 23).[1]

It is interesting to note that throughout his journey along the Circle of Consistence, Teilhard focused his attention on matter in all of its intricacy without much consideration of spirit. In fact, when he was young, the spirit world seemed quite elusive, a mere shadow of what was really real. On the other hand, he considered matter itself as divine (HM, 26)! The Divine Presence in which he felt himself bathed seemed to be not some vague spiritual entity, but rather, a supreme tangible reality (W, 128).

The study of physics propelled Teilhard into the cosmos. Its immense size and intricate structure amazed him. One can imagine him at night, sitting on the deck of a ship on its way to China looking up at the stars in amazement. On a clear night thousands of stars, the moon, and a few planets adorn the sky, but most structures are too far away to be seen with the naked eye. Like so many before him, Teilhard wanted to see beyond his own sight, whether the far away or the very small. He was always interested in technological advances that enhance our ability to see and would certainly be pleased to know of the increasingly sensitive optical instruments that today allow access to regions of space never before explored.

The telescope is perhaps the most fundamental of these instruments. From the time that Galileo plotted the orbits of the moons of Jupiter until the present day, it has enhanced both knowledge and enjoyment of the night sky. Optical telescopes with considerable power existed in Teilhard's day; some were even capable of distinguishing objects in galaxies outside our own. But, since then, the technology has improved dramatically, and much more has been discovered. Newer classes of telescopes help us to "see" in regions of the electromagnetic spectrum beyond the optical. And now that it is possible for telescopes to orbit Earth and to avoid the blurring caused by

---

[1] Thomas M. King, *Teilhard's Mysticism of Knowing* (New York: Seabury Press, 1981), 24.

Earth's atmosphere, our seeing power has greatly increased. Radio telescopes scan outer space looking for pulsars and quasars, measuring background microwave radiation, and hoping to detect signals coming from other forms of intelligent life on distant planets. X-ray telescopes detect radiation from binary stars and from black holes. The result is a raft of highly resolved optical images and beautiful false color images of nebulae as well as other deep-space structures.

Some telescopes probe a narrow pencil-like area of the sky so that they can focus on galaxies that are faint, while others focus on a broader region of space and concentrate on the brightest galaxies. Using data collected with these instruments, astrophysicists, hoping to determine the structure of the cosmos and to better understand its origins, have already mapped about one million galaxies. As a consequence, our knowledge of cosmic structure is growing by unimaginable proportions. Hundreds of billions of galaxies, each containing hundreds of billions of stars, are clumped in clusters and superclusters. Giant nebulae, filled with glowing gas and dust, contain the seeds of new stars. At the far distant reaches of space, very energetic galaxies called quasars exude huge amounts of radiation. In the 1920s, Edwin Hubble noticed that the universe is in fact expanding and that the speed at which the galaxies are moving away from our own Milky Way Galaxy depends on their distance from us. Today, measurements confirm not only that the cosmos is expanding, but also that galaxies are accelerating as they move away from each other.

Measuring devices such as computers, cameras, and spectroscopes enhance the telescope's potential to plumb both the grandeur and the immensity of space by collecting other sorts of data that shed light on the structure and composition of stars. These instruments give us new eyes and advance the notion of seeing to new dimensions. The spectrograph, for instance, measures and analyzes the wavelengths and intensity of the light coming from the stars and other celestial bodies and compares these findings with the spectra of elements found on Earth. Astrophysicists use this information to identify the elements that make up the stars and other deep space objects. They have noticed that elements found in outer space are the same as those present on Earth. Ordinary matter found both on Earth and in the stars is composed of intricate combinations of a handful of particles: protons, neutrons, and electrons; all matter, it seems, is essentially made from the same stuff.

However, in recent years it has become clear that only between 4 percent and 5 percent of the cosmic density is attributable to ordinary matter. The rest is quite elusive: about 25 percent of the cosmic density is due to dark matter, a little understood entity that is probably composed of as-yet-unknown exotic subatomic particles that hold the galaxies together gravitationally but do not interact with light. Dark matter is purported to have played a central role in the formation of cosmic structures such as galaxies. The other 70 percent of the cosmic density is due to dark energy. It is clear that dark energy behaves like a reverse gravity, causing a speeding up in the expansion of the universe.[2] What constitutes the elusive dark energy is still unknown. The precise makeup of dark matter and dark energy is one of the major open questions in astrophysics.

The spatial structure of the cosmos differs depending on the scale at which it is observed. On the largest cosmic scale, space seems to be homogeneous and isotropic; that is, galaxies seem to be scattered evenly like sifted sand, the same in every direction. On a somewhat smaller scale, structure begins to appear: galaxies, clusters of galaxies, superclusters of galaxies, and enormous bubble walls. In fact, great cobweb-like clusters of galaxies, such as the Great Wall and the Cetus Wall, are distributed in sheet-like structures each more than a billion light

---

[2] Joel Primack and Nancy Abrams, *View from the Center of the Universe: Discovering Our Extraordinary Place in the Cosmos* (New York: Riverhead Books, 2006), 99.

years long.[3] These long thin walls of super-galactic clusters surround huge voids or cosmic bubbles that were probably formed as galaxies collided in the early universe. Findings from recent observations of the microwave background radiation confirm that, although the early universe was fairly homogeneous, matter began quite early to form clumps,[4] probably because of quantum flux—the random occurrence of high density regions arising in the primordial material. As the universe expanded, any small inhomogeneity would have been magnified. It also appears that, in the early universe, matter might have first begun collecting in networks of thin filaments and that only later did those filaments coalesce into clusters and superclusters of galaxies.

At the other extreme, at the scale of the elementary particle, matter behaves according to the strange rules of quantum mechanics. What we usually call particles sometimes behave like waves, and waves sometime behave like particles. Matter behaves differently on the microscale where quantum mechanics prevails. At the heart of what appears to be empty space, the frenzied quantum foam bubbles up and elementary particles can become quite agitated. Confined to a small region of space, particles rattle around in that region at very high speeds. Furthermore, fluctuations at the quantum level blur the concept of the particle because, in an instant, what seemed like a pair of particles can be transformed into pure energy. In the quantum world particles come and go. Only the total energy of the universe remains constant. The fact that matter behaves so differently at the microscale where quantum mechanics operates and at the macroscale where gravity prevails causes difficulty for physicists who are trying to devise a unified theory that would simultaneously characterize the behavior of all four of the fundamental forces: gravitational, electromagnetic, and the strong and weak nuclear forces.

---

[3] Timothy Ferris, *The Whole Shebang: A State-of-the-Universe(s) Report* (New York: Simon and Schuster, 1997), 146, 152.

[4] Ibid., 34.

Not only has our understanding of the large-scale structure of the cosmos grown in magnitude, but our ability to view the inner physical structure of matter is also more finely tuned. Although sixty orders of magnitude separate the very largest cosmic structures from the very smallest,[5] present-day technology is improving our view of the world of the very small. Instruments such as the scanning tunneling microscope and the atomic force microscope are our eyes into the nanoworld. They provide a window that allows us to see more clearly down to the scale of the molecule and the atom. Using a stylus that is sharp enough to sense the shape of a particle on the atomic scale, the scanning tunneling microscope can determine the structure and size of an atom by sensing and recording amplitude variations on a sample's surface. A computer program then uses this information to reconstruct an image of the atom.[6]

In Teilhard's day the number of known elementary particles was small. Protons and neutrons were considered elementary. Now, we know that protons and neutrons are composed of quarks, particles that are still more elementary. Scientists continue to explore matter at the microscale and to speculate about its ultimate makeup, assuming that there is an ultimate elementary constituent. Several generations of particle accelerators have been probing the structure of matter by accelerating elementary particles to speeds close to the speed of light and then letting them collide. Often these experiments generate new particles so that the list of known particles continues to expand.

According to the standard model the total number of fundamental particles is twenty-eight. These are grouped in three categories: *quarks* that comprise mesons and baryons such as protons and neutrons, *leptons* such as electrons and muons, and *gauge bosons* such as photons that mediate the

---

[5] Primack and Abrams, *View from the Center of the Universe*, 160.

[6] Ted Sargent, *The Dance of Molecules: How Nanotechnology Is Changing Our Lives* (New York: Thunder's Mouth Press, 2006), 19.

electromagnetic force between charged particles and gluons that mediate the strong force between quarks. It is estimated today that there are more than 10^{79} protons in the universe, each identical to every other—all with the same charge, the same mass, the same properties. These particles become interesting and unique only when they are in relationship with other particles. Quarks bond to create neutrons and protons; neutrons and protons fuse to form nuclei; atoms join together forming many different types of molecules that in turn can form an even greater variety of polymers. In his magnum opus, *The Human Phenomenon*, Teilhard notes that relationship is at the heart of the creative universe. For Teilhard, "to be" is to be in relationship. Today, it has become clear that matter cannot exist unless it is in interaction. Interdependence, rather than independence, is the hallmark of the cosmos.

Recently, the Large Hadron Collider seems to have found evidence for the existence of the Higgs boson, a particularly elusive particle, whose existence is purported to explain why some elementary particles have mass. Located in a huge circular tunnel and buried in the Franco-Swiss border near Geneva, Switzerland, this gigantic particle accelerator is probing the inner reaches of matter more deeply than ever before. To determine the proton's structure, two proton beams are accelerated in opposite directions to very high energy by means of strong electric and magnetic fields. Once the particles have reached an energy level high enough so that they are traveling at a speed close to the speed of light, they collide head on. The remnants from the collisions are then scrutinized for new and interesting particles. Results from these and other experiments will probably continue to refine our ideas about the basic constituents of matter and might someday provide insight into the elusive dark matter.

Like Teilhard, physicists have been struggling for many years to understand what, at a most fundamental level, holds matter together. They claim to be searching for the "theory of everything," a theory that would "interweave all of nature's forces and material constituents within a single tapestry."[7] We now know of four forces that act to hold matter together: the gravitational force, the electromagnetic force, the weak force responsible for radioactive decay, and the strong nuclear force responsible for nuclear binding. However, very close to the beginning of time, in the extreme heat of the early universe, long before any large structures existed, these forces were indistinguishable. Now, they differ by many orders of magnitude, and depending on the scale of the phenomenon, one of these forces usually predominates. At the level of the planet and up to the cosmic level, gravity is the dominant force holding together individual stars, star systems, and galaxies. The electromagnetic force is responsible for chemical bonding and, therefore, for holding atoms and molecules together. The strong and weak nuclear forces are operational at the level of the atomic nucleus, where the strong force holds the particles in the nucleus together.

The modern approach to the unification of nature's forces began in the late nineteenth century with Michael Faraday, who first suggested that the effects of forces can be better visualized when they are represented in terms of fields. A field is essentially a map that indicates a particle's strength and the direction of the sphere of its influence, or when there are many particles, the strength and direction of the sphere of influence of the group of particles as a whole. Because of the field's long-range behavior, it is difficult to localize a particle, to say exactly where the particle that the field represents begins and where it ends. Fields make it clear that the particle's influence and thus its identity reach well beyond the particle's material structure. Massive particles attract other massive particles that are within their field of influence; positively charged particles repel other positively charged particles; the

---

[7] Brian Greene, *The Elegant Universe: Superstrings, Hidden Dimensions, and the Quest for the Ultimate Theory* (New York: Vintage Books: 1999), 4.

strength of the field that surrounds a particle determines the strength and extent of its influence.

Teilhard was struck by the unity and interconnection he observed within the world of matter. He notes: "The farther and deeper we penetrate into matter with our increasingly powerful methods, the more dumbfounded we are by the interconnection of its parts" (HP, 14). Today, as technology responsible for seeing into the hidden depths of matter improves, this statement seems truer than ever. In fact, elements no longer seem either solid or particulate. Instead, as quantum mechanics and superstring theory show, they are interactive, always on the move, and ever ready to relate.[8]

In the late nineteenth century, James Clerk Maxwell noticed that electric fields and magnetic fields behave in a symmetric way; moving charges generate magnetic fields, and moving magnets cause electric fields. Using this fact he was able to integrate the known laws of electricity and magnetism into a single electromagnetic theory. In the early twentieth century, Albert Einstein developed the theory of special relativity by weaving together space and time. Then, in his theory of general relativity, he wove gravity into the spacetime fabric, replacing the mechanistic Newtonian view of space, time, and gravity with a geometric and more dynamic description.[9] In the presence of a massive body Einstein's spacetime warps the way a waterbed does if a bowling ball rests on it. This warping in turn affects the dynamics of objects moving in its vicinity. Just as the path of a ball rolling down an ice-covered slope is determined by the curvature of the slope, so the curvature of spacetime influences the motion of objects near massive bodies. The warping of spacetime by a massive body explains not only the motion of the planets as they orbit the sun but also the

---

[8] This and what follows is adapted from my lecture "The Texture of Ultimate Reality and Teilhard's Cosmic Tapestry," Metanexus Institute, Philadelphia, September 25, 2002.

[9] Greene, *The Elegant Universe*, 75–76.

deflection of light as it traverses the rippled fabric in the neighborhood of a massive body. This influence is reciprocal. The presence of spinning and colliding massive objects can also cause spacetime to twist and to wrinkle. Dissatisfied with the partial synthesis that he created, Einstein spent the rest of his life trying to integrate electromagnetism with his theory of general relativity. Although he never fulfilled this dream of formulating a true "theory of everything," its pursuit has continued to challenge physicists who have come after him.

During the decade of the 1970s further attempts at integration proved successful as the electromagnetic and the weak and strong nuclear forces were woven together in the Grand Unified Theory (GUT). At interparticle distances of about a hundredth of a billionth of a billionth of a billionth of a centimeter, called the Planck length, these three non-gravitational forces become equal in strength.[10] However, including the gravitational force in this scheme continues to be a challenge.

Most recently, those searching for unification have adopted superstring theory as a potential candidate. This theory attempts to integrate Einstein's theory of general relativity, which treats the effect of the gravitational force on objects on the cosmic scale, with quantum mechanics, which treats very small-scale phenomena at the elementary particle level. To achieve this merger, superstring theorists begin with the assumption that each matter particle consists of an infinitesimal, vibrating string—an oscillating, dancing filament[11] that harmonizes and provides the ultimate cosmic music at the deepest level of matter.[12] These strings, if they exist, are of the

---

[10] Ibid., 177.

[11] Ibid., 14.

[12] For an expanded treatment of Teilhard's use of the tapestry metaphor, see Kathleen Duffy, "The Texture of the Evolutionary Cosmos," *Teilhard Studies* 43 (Fall 2001); idem, "The Texture of the Evolutionary Cosmos: Matter and Spirit in Teilhard de Chardin," in *Teilhard in the Twenty-first Century: The Emerging Spirit of the Earth*, ed. Arthur Fabel, Donald St. John (Maryknoll, NY: Orbis Books, 2003), 138–53.

order of the Planck length, which is about fourteen orders of magnitude smaller than the atom, so they are invisible even to our most powerful optical devices. Their extensions in spacetime become infinitely narrow tubes, causing the Planck scale to exhibit plenty of structure.

The resonant, vibrational patterns of a particle's internal string determine properties, such as mass and charge, which differentiate it from every other particle. These twisting and vibrating strings interact with one another through the phenomenon of resonance, which causes them to knit together and fall apart. Brian Greene visualizes these tiny superstrings as the threads of an elusive tapestry, whose vibrational patterns actually "orchestrate the evolution of the cosmos."[13] As strings resonate and interact, they weave the fabric of spacetime, a fabric that is warped and rippled by gravitational forces, one that undergoes extreme contortions and, in the process, is able to tear and repair itself. Because the scale at which superstrings operate is so much smaller than that of the atom, it has been hard to imagine an experiment that will verify their existence directly, especially given today's technology. However, scientists continue to develop indirect methods of testing the validity of superstring theory, especially at the cosmic scale.

One of the strange consequences of the unification provided by superstring theory is that it requires that spacetime be composed of eleven dimensions rather than the familiar four dimensions of Einstein's spacetime. While four of these dimensions are, like Einstein's spacetime dimensions, large, extended, and directly manifest, the other seven dimensions are so small that they can be curled up ("compactified") into the folded fabric of the cosmos, making them invisible to macroscopic measurements. Nevertheless, these seven extra dimensions, though tiny and invisible, determine in large measure the fundamental properties of the universe.

---

[13] Greene, *The Elegant Universe*, 5, 135.

Scientists continue to explore the consequences of general relativity. They realize that the sudden motion of a massive body will cause gravity waves to ripple through the fabric of spacetime. Facilities such as the Laser Interferometer Gravitational-Wave Observatory (LIGO) provide new windows into the cosmic fabric and will eventually enable us to "hear" and "feel" these vibrations. Once LIGO begins detecting gravity waves, we will be able to hear "the cymbal crashes from exploding stars, periodic drumbeats from a swiftly rotating pulsar, an extended glissando—a rapid ride up the scale—from the merger of two black holes, as well as a faint background hiss, the gravitational equivalent of the cosmic microwave background."[14]

In conjunction with his work as geologist and paleontologist, Teilhard spent many hours exploring rock formations. He had a keen interest in the structure of Earth's lithosphere as a whole and in determining how the various layers of rock formed over time. One of his tasks as a stratigrapher was to classify rock formations into their constituent layers and to identify the composition and age of each layer. Thus, he was primed to think of Earth in layers.

Geologists continue to represent Earth's overall structure as a series of layers or concentric spherical shells: The barysphere, which consists of Earth's core and lower mantle, is surrounded by the lithosphere, which contains the upper mantle and Earth's crust. The lithosphere, in turn, is surrounded by the hydrosphere, which comprises the oceans that cover about 71 percent of Earth's surface; many smaller bodies of water such as rivers, streams, and lakes; the water in solid, liquid, and vapor form that is trapped in the atmosphere; and ice frozen in glaciers. Meteorologists divide Earth's atmosphere into the troposphere, the stratosphere, and the mesosphere. Teilhard eventually extended his strong

---

[14] See Marcia Bartusiak, *Einstein's Unfinished Symphony: Listening to the Sounds of Spacetime* (New York: Penguin Putnam, 2003), 153.

interest in the structure of Earth's lithosphere to the structure and texture of the biosphere. This layer contains the variety of living organisms that populate Earth, the most complex forms of matter known today.

Teilhard continued to focus on rock, especially on details about the formation of the variety of structures that matter in the lithosphere assumed over Earth's lifetime. Here again the bonding process used to form glasses and crystals interested him. Unlike glasses such as obsidian, which form too quickly to crystalize, a crystal forms in a very simple way and displays an amazing symmetry. Once its seed forms, the bulk crystal grows by juxtaposing relatively uncomplicated atoms or molecules to its surface, layer by layer, so that they form a geometrical lattice (HP, 35). Bonded together by electric forces, the atoms or molecules in the seed crystal tend to attract other atoms or molecules, encouraging them to line up so that the initial pattern repeats itself indefinitely. Eventually the crystal develops a long-range static order. This gives the crystal great beauty of shape but not much spontaneity.

Teilhard compared the relative simplicity of the crystal with the greater complexity of the polymer. He noted that a crystal displays long-range order but has no center of unity. When crystals break in two, each part retains its identity as a particular crystal. On the other hand, polymers, the large carbon-based organic molecules that are important to all life, form in an entirely different way. Covalent bonds join smaller molecules, which link together in chains or strings that cannot break apart without destroying the polymer itself. The same is true to an even greater degree for all biological structures: cells and organisms, plants and animals. Each biological structure is greater than the sum of its parts and exhibits properties in the whole that are not present in the parts. When biological structures break apart, they lose their unique properties.

At an early age Teilhard began to be bothered by the poignant reality that, in the biosphere, things fall apart and die. The flowers that gave him joy, withered (W, 126); flames in his fireplace burned up a lock of his hair; soldiers died in battle during the war; some of his own siblings died at an early age. It was particularly difficult for Teilhard, who longed to find "the stable, the unfailing, the absolute," to experience things crumbling (W, 124). As he considered the immensity of the cosmos and the fragility of living things, his initial response was to assume that, since living things fall apart, he mattered little. Imagining himself as a simple particle adrift in the vastness of the universe, he experienced the kind of distress that such a worldview causes (D, 78). However, zoology and paleontology were pivots (HM, 22) that turned Teilhard toward the biosphere. He did eventually become interested in living organisms—in the beauty of the flower and the strength of the beetle—even though these were so clearly perishable (HM, 22). At first, he reconciled his love for plants and animals by renaming the fragile and perishable as the new and exotic. But eventually his eyes acquired a new sensitivity:

> This crumbling away, which is the mark of the corruptible and the precarious, is to be seen everywhere. And yet everywhere there are traces of, and a yearning for, a unique support, a unique and absolute soul, a unique reality in which other realities are brought together in synthesis, as stable and universal as matter, as simple as spirit. (W, 124)

At last Teilhard began to "distinguish in the Universe a *profound*, essential *Unity*, a unity burdened with imperfections . . . but a real unity within which every 'chosen' substance gains increasing solidity" (HM, 199).

Teilhard's experience of the cosmic structure was intimate, intricate, and profound. He began to see himself as part of an interdependent and interconnected reality, sharing the one life that is in everything.[15] He realized that if he kept looking for consistency in outward appearances—in the life of a single

---

[15] Dorothee Soelle, *The Silent Cry: Mysticism and Resistance* (Minneapolis: Fortress Press, 2001), 214.

flower, for instance—he would continue to be disappointed. Instead, he began to see "the very consistency of the World . . . welling up . . . like sap, through every fibre . . . leaping up like a flame" (HM, 34). Divine Presence, so powerfully real to him as he traveled along the first circle, had acquired a new power for him. At the very heart of matter, Divine Consistence was, by its very presence, holding all things together. Once he became aware of "the unifying influence of the universal Presence" (W, 124), he was no longer distressed by the mutability of things: "Beneath what is temporal and plural, the mystic can see only the unique Reality which is the support common to all substances, and which clothes and dyes itself in all the universe's countless shades without sharing their impermanence" (W, 125). He knew that Divine Consistence is trustworthy (W, 123): "Having come face to face with a universal and enduring reality to which one can attach those fragmentary moments of happiness that . . . excite the heart without satisfying it" (W, 124), "a glorious, unsuspected feeling of joy invaded my soul" (W, 126). He longed to surrender, to drive his roots into matter so that he could become united with Ultimate Reality.

4.

The Circle of Energy

Amid the complexity and immobility of the rocks
there rise suddenly toward me "gusts of being,"
sudden and brief fits of awareness of the laborious
unification of things,
and it is no longer myself thinking, but the Earth
acting.

—Pierre Teilhard de Chardin,
Letters to Two Friends 1926–1952, 73

Touched by the intricate and beautiful structure of the cosmos and yearning to be possessed by the Sacred Presence that fills it (W, 128), Teilhard continued his mystical journey, ever searching for the supreme tangible reality. As he stepped into the third circle, he found the cosmos ablaze with activity. The Divine Presence that had been alluring him had suddenly acquired a new aspect—Energy.

Teilhard's field work as geologist and paleontologist immersed him in Earth's landscape. Despite their apparent rigidity, he was able to read in Earth's rocky layers a story of tremendous change and great creativity. In the strata of rock and the fossil record that he explored, he found evidence for the dynamic and ever-changing process that had quite recently been discovered by the world of science and whose full implications were only beginning to be noticed. This put a tangible face on the theory of evolution and helped him to imagine events that happened thousands or millions or even billions of years ago. A fast-forwarded evolutionary view of Earth's more than four-billion-year history highlighted Earth's profound fluidity and plasticity. This convinced him not only of the validity of the theory of evolution but also of its creative potential. The more he thought about evolution as it applied to life on Earth and to the cosmos as a whole, the more he became aware of Energy hidden within matter: "The light will emerge only when we go deeper. We shall see its radiance only if we leave behind the outer husk of beings and succeed in discovering what is hidden deep down in them" (S, 23). From the moment that evolution revealed itself to him, Teilhard's mysticism depended in a fundamental way on the power of the evolutionary story.

When Teilhard first learned about the theory of evolution, so little data were available that its mechanisms were still a mystery. Our present understanding and confidence in the theory is far superior. Deeper understanding of the evolution of life on Earth due to processes of natural selection and genetic mutation, as well as of the evolution of matter and energy due to gravitational, electromagnetic, and nuclear forces, provides richer details about the cosmic story. Scientists tell us that the universe began almost fourteen billion years ago with a primordial flaring forth of highly compressed energy, in an event that is popularly called the Big Bang. During the first few minutes, matter in the form of elementary particles emerged, and in the heat of the early universe, helium was produced from the fusion of protons and neutrons. Within the first few million years gas and dust particles scattered throughout space began clustering in clumps and eventually developed into galaxies, each composed of billions of stars. Within the stellar cores extremely high temperatures forged new elements such as carbon, oxygen, and nitrogen. After many millions of years, when the largest of these stars depleted their fuel and were no longer able to carry on the fusion process in their cores, they exploded as supernovas, scattering their newly formed elements into space. The resultant enriched gas and dust became the raw material for second- and third-generation star systems. Our sun, with its planets and their moons, as well as many asteroids and comets, was created from the remnants of such a supernova. Soon after it was formed, our Earth developed a protective atmosphere, and its surface eventually became more stable.

The emergence of the biosphere some four billion years ago is an important critical point in Earth's history. Teilhard was particularly enthralled whenever he thought about the way living, organic matter emerged from inorganic matter. At this major turning point in the complexification of matter, suddenly, as if passing through a phase transition, the world became lustrous; a new dimension appeared in Earth's surface layer. The biosphere was born. As Teilhard contemplated Earth's story and watched matter come alive, he experienced a deep sense of awe: "See how [Earth's] shades are changing. From age to age its colors intensify. Something is going to burst out on the juvenile Earth. Life! See, it is life!" (HP, 38). Teilhard began to understand the significance of Earth's unifying properties in a new way: "When we reach the cell," he said, "these properties have definitely emerged, and we feel that we are moving into a different world" (A, 33). Throughout the last four billion years, more and more complex life forms have evolved from simple one-celled organisms to produce the variety of plants and animals that we now find on Earth. Having emerged probably only within the last few hundred thousand years, the human species as we know it today is a latecomer to Earth's long history.

Details about the cosmic story have been collected with the aid of telescopes. Focused on deep space, these powerful instruments actually allow us to look back in time and collect light that has been traveling from faraway objects for many years. The distance to quasars, for example, is so large that it takes approximately thirteen billion years for light from these bright objects to arrive on Earth. Since it takes millions of years for a star to form, to live a productive life, and then to die, it is impossible to follow the long life history of a single star in real time. Viewing a star through a telescope over many years provides a series of snapshots that covers too short a time span to learn about that star's long life history. However, we can observe stars and galaxies at various developmental stages—as protostars, as fully-developed stars, as supernovas, as planetary nebulae, as white dwarfs, as neutron stars, and as black holes. Astrophysicists are able to piece together these snapshots and reconstruct the steps in the life cycles of various types of stars. They can determine to high precision the conditions of the universe throughout cosmic history and determine how the universe has evolved.

Because the cosmic evolutionary process has been happening over a very long time, it is difficult to imagine the many aspects that characterize its development and to grasp their underlying dynamics in a single moment. To observe the cosmos as a whole and to appreciate its nature, it would be helpful to have a map, a concise way to visualize at a glance the gradual cosmic forward movement. In some ways this map would be similar to a conductor's score. Because it is impossible to hear a symphony as a whole at any one moment in time, composers create a musical score that in principle contains all of the elements needed to reconstruct the symphony. The score provides for the musician a map of the symphony's rich unfolding.

To provide a map of the cosmic becoming, Teilhard has suggested plotting the activity of the cosmos in four-dimensional spacetime, offering a visual though mathematical representation for a process that can be experienced only in time. Teilhard visualized a graph starting close to the beginning of time after elementary particles burst forth from the energy of the original cosmic singularity like fireworks. An array of points representing these particles would be scattered randomly on a three-dimensional plot (HP, 17). As time moves forward, each particle traces out a thread-like curve that interacts with many of the other threads. As each particle wanders among the others, it weaves a four-dimensional tapestry in this cosmic plot. As the electromagnetic force causes protons to repel, the threads move apart. Then, since the protons are energized enough to come close together, the strong nuclear force is capable of fusing them and thus producing a new element, deuterium, also known as heavy hydrogen. As protons continue to fuse into deuterium and then, through more complex interactions, into tritium, helium, carbon, and a raft of other light elements, knots form in the tapestry giving it texture (W, 21). Sometimes the knots fall apart and the individual threads interact once again, reemerging as something altogether new. Sometimes they join other knots to form more intricate knots. As time progresses, the weaving continues as particles relate with one another in more complex ways.

As the universe begins to expand and cool, nuclei attract electrons and form atoms. Later, atoms search for partners and form a variety of molecules, which then unite with other molecules to form polymers, the building blocks for cells. A profusion of cells converges and provides the impetus for the formation of an exorbitant number of organisms, providing the basis for life on Earth. The human species has emerged as the most recent product of Earth's evolutionary process. At each step of this ever-complexifying process, the threads of the cosmic tapestry become more flexible and more spontaneous, so that the number of possible outcomes of the weaving process grows exponentially. Each new complexity prepares the way for still richer and more complex forms.

This tapestry is Teilhard's visual model of evolutionary behavior, his map of the cosmic becoming. It highlights, in a way that is difficult to portray otherwise, the amazing energy at work at the heart of the cosmos and models beautifully not only the interconnectedness and interdependence of all matter but also matter's inclination toward union: "endless and untearable, so closely woven in one piece that there is not one single knot in it that does not depend upon the whole fabric" (S, 79). The tapestry presents a holistic and integrated picture of the ceaseless process that has been at work for billions of years. It transforms what seemed, at first, to be a sea of cosmic particles into an evolving network whose threads continue to weave in and out of spacetime as they interact with one another, create new entities, and fall apart. Eventually, the elementary particles that had once swarmed in the heat of the early universe respond to forces that encourage complexity, originality, and beauty, and commit themselves to relationships that are more or less complex.

Teilhard noticed that something profound has been happening in the cosmos since the beginning of time—the complex is gradually emerging from the union of simpler structures. In fact, a thrust toward union seems to be coded into the very fabric of the cosmos. On each level of the cosmic hierarchy, a bonding process exists that tends to create new entities. He called this general pattern by which more centered, more complex forms emerge in the evolutionary universe "Creative Union,"[1] pointing out that complexity arises at all levels because of the propensity of matter to develop intimate relationships. The threads of the cosmic tapestry are thus encouraged to experiment with ever more innovative patterns.

One of the earliest examples of Creative Union involves the fusion process. Fusion happens when the protons, neutrons, and other light nuclei found in the early atmosphere of the Big Bang and later in the cores of the stars bond to form heavier nuclei. Although nuclei are positively charged and naturally repel one another, in environments of extremely high temperature and pressure, such as those found in the core of a star, these particles are highly energized. As they move at very high speed in the plasma environment of the stellar core, they are often able to come close enough to feel and respond to the attractive, short-range, strong nuclear force. When they do, they fuse and form a stable nucleus. In the process they release

---

[1] Sion Cowell, *The Teilhard Lexicon: Understanding the Language, Terminology, and Vision of the Writings of Pierre Teilhard de Chardin* (Portland, OR: Sussex Academic Press, 2001), 205.

a tremendous amount of energy. Transformed into elements with properties very different from those of the original nuclei, the end products of the fusion process are then capable of further complexification.

The process of Creative Union, the desire and tendency in nature to become more, has been driving the evolutionary process from the beginning. It has been keeping nature in search of new ways to adapt to the changing environment. This process impressed Teilhard. He noted that whenever elements do interact and unite, they become something new with greater potential. He describes this phenomenon succinctly: "union differentiates" (HP, 186). When elements unite they become more than they were by themselves as they participate in a higher form of being. Examples of this abound: water molecules have properties different from those of the hydrogen and oxygen atoms from which they are formed; the union of sperm with egg generates a zygote that, in both form and potential, is quite unlike the components from which the new cell is made.

Creative Union, the process of producing more complex elements from simpler ones, provides for the continual emergence of cosmic novelty. For Teilhard, Creative Union takes matter, which he defines as anything that is capable of being united, and complexifies it, forming a new whole (HM, 227). Matter continues to become more whenever it unites with more (S, 45); in fact, matter cannot exist without interacting, and it cannot become something new without uniting. As Teilhard notes, "The richness of a creature depends on the perfection of its form . . . and on the value of the collective . . . forms that use the creature to build up higher degrees of union in the Universe" (HM, 229).

Like Teilhard, complexity scientists have recently been asking how things hold together. Struck by the beauty of structures as diverse as spiral galaxies, the colorful and intricate patterns on butterfly wings, and the social behavior of insects, they are interested in describing mathematically how organisms evolve and why certain structures exist. Because living organisms, like all complex systems, are open to the environment, they tend to be spontaneous, disorderly, and alive. They somehow manage to adapt, to reorganize themselves, to produce exquisitely tuned patterns, and constantly to transcend themselves. Together, they acquire collective properties such as life, thought, and purpose that they could never have possessed on their own.[2]

Because the fate of a complex system is so profoundly intertwined with its environment, its study requires a treatment that is more holistic than that which had generally been practiced in the sciences.[3] To avoid dealing with the complications that the environment exerts on a physical system, scientists, until recently, focused on linear systems that are isolated from their environments. As much as possible, parameters such as temperature, pressure, and volume were kept constant or at least controlled during an experiment. This was done for practical reasons. The environment often introduces nonlinear effects that make the equations that model the process difficult to solve. Physical processes that involve turbulence were often ignored. Before the advent of the computer, more complicated physical systems, particularly nonlinear systems, were too difficult to solve analytically. Thus, scientists focused on a small subset of physical problems that were actually solvable. Yet, avoiding the difficult case of turbulence as if it were an exception and ignoring complex and chaotic behavior has led to the expectation of a spectrum of physical outcomes that is too narrow. Today, however, with the advance in high-speed computers, it is possible to study systems that are far from equilibrium and, in some cases, to include environmental effects. Complexity scientists are now searching for an overriding set of rules that will generate the stable, yet flexible,

---

[2] M. Mitchell Waldrop, *Complexity: The Emerging Science at the Edge of Order and Chaos* (New York: Simon and Schuster, 1992), 11–12.

[3] The section that follows is adapted from Kathleen Duffy, "The Texture of the Evolutionary Cosmos," *Teilhard Studies* 43 (Fall 2001).

creativity found in nature.[4] Using new mathematical language and techniques, they are discovering that when a few simple rules are applied to a variety of complex systems, intricate patterns begin to emerge.

Unlike complex systems, chaotic systems are generally simple. However, because they are nonlinear and influenced by positive feedback, they respond in complex ways. Although chaotic systems are deterministic, that is, governed by universal physical laws and not by chance, they are extremely sensitive to the environment. A small change in energy input or in the initial values of a system's variables generates an entirely new response. This makes predicting the future of a chaotic system quite difficult.

Graphs help scientists to see, to analyze, and to understand a system's dynamics. A particularly helpful type of graph often used to explore chaotic behavior is the phase diagram. On a phase diagram the variables that describe the evolving state of a system are plotted in a space that contains as many dimensions as there are variables. For instance, an oscillating pendulum bob can be described by two variables: its angular position and its angular velocity. The pendulum bob's orbit, constructed by plotting the instantaneous angular velocity of its mass vs. its angular position, provides insight into the behavior of the pendulum. If there is no friction to damp out the pendulum's energy, its motion is regular, and an elliptical phase plot called a limit cycle results. The pendulum's constant shape represents the orderly behavior of a dependable, periodic process that continually repeats itself. If the pendulum's motion is over-damped, as it would be if the pendulum bob were immersed in molasses, its orbit will spiral in to a stable point. This kind of attractor is called a fixed point, since every set of initial conditions will eventually lead to the same final state of rest.

A chaotic pendulum, on the other hand, can execute fairly complex dynamics. To produce chaotic pendulum motion, one

---

[4] Stephen Wolfram, *A New Kind of Science* (Champaign, IL: Wolfram Media, 2002), 21.

could place a pendulum bob in a viscous fluid and attach it by a cable to an oscillating beam. For certain values of viscosity and oscillation frequency, the bob executes chaotic motion. Although always remaining attached to the oscillating beam, the chaotic pendulum never repeats a cycle in exactly the same way, making it impossible to predict its motion. Despite the tendency of the pendulum bob to wander in a way that might at first seem erratic, order is nevertheless maintained. The chaotic pendulum is capable of producing a collection of profoundly intricate and beautiful orbits, each depending on the available input energy and on the amount of energy dissipated by the viscous fluid. Called strange attractors, chaotic orbits embody intricate yet unpredictable order.

Chaotic behavior requires that at least two opposing forces act on a system simultaneously—one force, such as friction, dissipates energy, while another force, such as gravity, supplies the energy needed to keep the system far from equilibrium. One force works to stabilize the system; the other works to destabilize it. The overall result is that driving the system far from equilibrium makes it capable of creating new structures while avoiding thermal disorder.

Scientists are studying a variety of physical systems that exhibit chaotic behavior. Earth's atmosphere experiences an intricate interplay of the energy-producing force of gravity and the dissipative force of convection. When plotted in a certain way, atmospheric state variables such as temperature and pressure exhibit the well-known Lorenz attractor, often called the butterfly attractor because of the shape of its orbit. Voltage drops across elements in circuits made up of nonlinear elements exhibit chaotic orbits when they are displayed on an oscilloscope screen. A low temperature fluid trapped in a Bénard convection cell between two flat plates exhibits regular hexagonal convection cells when driven far from equilibrium.[5] A fluid trapped between two concentric cylinders

    [5] Gregoire Nicolis and Ilya Prigogine, *Exploring Complexity: An Introduction* (New York: W. H. Freeman, 1989), 13, 15.

that are rotating in opposite directions relative to each other produces, for certain values of the rotational velocity, an intricately patterned flow.[6] Another interesting complex system with a dramatic response is the chemical clock generated in the Belousov-Zhabotinskii reaction. This reaction is produced by dissolving cesium sulphate, malonic acid, and potassium bromide in sulfuric acid. The reagents are continually pumped into the solution to keep it well mixed. Red dye is used to indicate an excess presence of Ce^{3+} ions and blue dye an excess of Ce^{4+} ions. When the pumping rate is increased so that the solution is driven far from equilibrium, an amazing change occurs. Instead of the blurred violet mixture that one might expect, the solution changes from red to blue approximately every two minutes. Unlike a pendulum clock, which depends on gravity to keep it going, this clock depends on the internal dynamical activity of the reaction and especially positive feedback. In fact, it seems that these highly coherent molecules are able to "communicate" over large distances.[7]

Living systems are complex systems because they also experience two opposing forces: self-organization and natural selection. Self-organization is the energy-enhancing process; natural selection, is the limiting process.[8] Together these processes maintain the complex order so evident in living systems.

The chaotic dynamics of natural processes produce fractal structures whose irregular fluid boundaries are unlike machine-made objects with straight edges and parallel lines. The turbulent flow of air in the atmosphere generates fractal cloud patterns from condensing water vapor; over millennia,

---

[6] James Gleick, *Chaos: Making a New Science* (New York: Viking Penguin, 1987), 128–31.

[7] Brian Goodwin, *How the Leopard Changed Its Spots: The Evolution of Complexity* (New York: Simon and Schuster, 1994), 45.

[8] Stuart Kauffman, *At Home in the Universe: The Search for the Laws of Self-Organization and Complexity* (New York: Oxford University Press, 1995), 8, 112.

buffeting winds and rain produce the jagged surface features characteristic of mountains; turbulent oceans form irregular coastlines; the violent pumping of blood by the heart fashions a fractal blood stream. The surf-pounded coastline, the blood vessels of the heart (a very violent pump), and the wind- and rain-buffeted mountain exhibit fractal shapes. These graceful and artistically appealing shapes are formed by the interplay of powerful forces that drive them and strong damping forces that tend to subdue them. Because of the aggressive nature of both types of force, the resulting fractal shapes often turn out to be quite robust.[9] Fractal structures are interesting not only because they are self-similar, that is, they repeat a character-istic pattern on many different size scales, but also because they reside in a space of non-integer dimension, defying the ordinary Euclidean integer dimensions.

The formation of a strange attractor is often compared to the formation of eddies that arise in a mountain lake. In mountainous regions gravity exerts an attractive force on the water in the rivers and streams and drives it, sometimes at great speeds, down the mountainside to a nearby lake.[10] Once in the lake an incoming stream interacts with the lake environment, and because of forces such as convection, it often forms complex spiral patterns called eddies. The cur-rents that run through evolution behave in a similar fashion. Teilhard imagined the process of evolution in a way that is consonant with the formation of these strange attractors. Rather than pursuing a "gentle drift toward equilibrium," evolution creates an "irresistible 'Vortex' which spins into itself, always in the same direction . . . from the most simple to the most complex; spinning it into ever more . . . astro-nomically complicated [patterns]" (HM, 33). Evolution is truly dynamic: "From time to time these currents collide

---

[9] Clifford A. Pickover, *The Loom of God: Mathematical Tapestries at the Edge of Time* (New York: Plenum Publishing, 1997), 120–21.

[10] Kauffman, *At Home in the Universe*, 78.

with one another in formidable crises which cause them to seethe and foam in their efforts to establish their equilibrium" (W, 222).

The transition region that exists between ordered stability and chaotic instability is called the edge of chaos. In this particularly creative region, complex order abounds. On the brink between order and chaos, systems tend to fall apart and reorder themselves in more complex ways. Because a complex system is somewhat unstable, it is able to interact with its environment. As it does, dissipative and energy-enriching forces compete to form stable structures. Order emerges where one might have expected turbulence.

Complex systems often display coherent behavior. An example of this occurs in a Bénard convection cell in which a low-temperature fluid is trapped between two flat plates, one heated at the bottom to sustain a constant temperature difference. Driving the fluid far from equilibrium by increasing the difference in temperature between the plates to a critical value sets up a convection pattern in the fluid. As the temperature difference approaches a critical value, millions of molecules begin to move coherently, forming hexagonal convection cells of a characteristic size.[11] These patterns are absent at smaller values of the temperature gradient. For temperature gradients above the critical value, the fluid becomes turbulent. Unlike an ordinary fluid, whose molecules seem to move independently and usually interact only through short-range intermolecular forces, chaotic fluids experience interparticle correlations that are long range.[12] Highly coherent molecules act as if they are communicating with one another; even though these molecules are situated at relatively large distances from one another, they seem to know what the other is doing and respond accordingly.

---

[11] Ilya Prigogine and Isabelle Stengers, *Order Out of Chaos: Man's New Dialogue with Nature* (New York: Bantam Books, 1984), 142.

[12] Nicolis and Prigogine, *Exploring Complexity*, 13, 15.

Teilhard was fascinated by complexity. He lamented the fact that, in his day, physics ignored it. He considered complexity as a third infinite along with the infinitesimal and the immense: "The gap between the extreme of simplicity and the extreme of complexity is as astronomically great as that between stellar and atomic magnitudes" (T, 166). He felt that complexity could provide a way "to connect the phenomena of life—consciousness, freedom, inventive power—to the phenomena of nonliving matter: in other words, to find a natural place for biology as part of physics" (T, 167). He considered complexity as a state variable and suggested that one way to quantify complexity is simply to count the number of elements in combination. Today, there are many more sophisticated methods for quantifying the complexity of a system but still no standard approach.

To explore nature's creative processes, complexity scientist Stephen Wolfram writes computer programs known as cellular automata. He has been able to find sets of rules that he asserts reproduce the characteristic complex behavior of many physical systems.[13] Computer-generated output from countless experiments demonstrate that complexity is a normal outcome for these systems. Wolfram claims that his models are generating "a new kind of science" that will be powerful enough to encompass the results of traditional science and, as a byproduct, provide more physical insight into these and more complex phenomena. In particular, he suggests using cellular automata to model the behavior of the known universe in a way that is consistent with the laws of physics.[14]

The simplest cellular automaton consists of an initial line of squares colored either black or white (known as the initial conditions) plus a set of rules that determines the colors of

---

[13] Wolfram, *A New Kind of Science*, 466.

[14] This section and what follows is adapted from Kathleen Duffy, "The Cellular Automaton and the Cosmic Tapestry: Wolfram and Teilhard Model the Universe," in *Teilhard Perspectives* 37, no. 2 (Fall 2004). Also available online.

the cells in subsequent lines. The rules usually rely on local information such as the color of the cell itself and that of its closest neighbors. A typical rule might read: If a particular cell and its two neighbors are white, color the cell at that position on the next line black; otherwise color it white. After several iterations of the specified set of rules, a pattern often begins to appear that can be characterized as repetitive, nesting, random, or static.[15] With more complex initial conditions and carefully chosen rules for proceeding, computer scientists are learning how intricate patterns form. Wolfram has also devised a second generation of such programs called causal networks. These allow for the inclusion of time dependence and are characterized by a collection of nodes, which represent events, and a set of connections, which represents the causal relation between events.[16] In this formalism, the properties of a system depend critically on the ways in which the nodes are connected.[17]

Wolfram images the universe as a giant computer program that began from an initial state and has been responding to a set of embedded rules.[18] To propagate his model, he combines an automaton that updates the system in time with a causal network that describes relationships in space.[19] In fact, with a variety of cellular automata and causal networks, he claims that he is able to model not only spacetime but also gravity, relativity, and elementary particle interactions, and to fulfill the prescriptions of physical laws such as the conservation of energy, the second law of thermodynamics, and quantum mechanics. However, he notes how difficult, if not impossible, it is to decipher the rules simply from the patterns that we see in nature.[20] Although Wolfram has been able to generate

---

[15] Wolfram, *A New Kind of Science*, 106.
[16] Ibid., 490.
[17] Ibid., 193.
[18] Ibid., 434.
[19] Ibid., 475, 508.
[20] Ibid., 31.

the characteristic behavior of many physical systems, he notes that it will be impossible to find a simple rule for the universe as a whole or to know the ultimate outcome of the evolutionary project. In fact, he says that although "the wonders of our universe can in effect be captured by simple rules . . . there can be no way to know all the consequences of these rules, except to watch and see how they unfold."[21]

Both Teilhard and the complexity scientists underscore the fact that local interactions have global consequences. Wolfram's cellular automata show clearly that "local rules generate global order."[22] Rules that usually involve only nearest neighbors somehow affect the system as a whole. Teilhard also senses the far-reaching consequences of nearest neighbor interactions: "We have gradually come to understand that no elemental thread in the universe is wholly independent . . . of its neighboring threads" (F, 87). Just as the simplest vibration of a single cosmic tapestry thread affects the whole fabric, so local interactions can be felt on a global scale.

Like Wolfram, Teilhard considered deep connectivity and interdependence as basic elements of the cosmic program. He insisted that, when studying science, it is important to consider the whole of the phenomenon and not simply its parts (HP, 1). He notes that because "the multiple is bound together into the coherence of one solid whole" (W, 49), the cosmos cannot be reduced to its constituent parts without destroying its essence. In fact, "to fully define the nature of each element of the Cosmos . . . we have to consider . . . the pleiad . . . of which it is a participating member" (HM, 228–29). Although he was unable to provide scientific proof, he was aware that "deep down, there is in the substance of the cosmos a primordial disposition . . . for self-arrangement and self-involution" (HM, 33), and that if the vast disorder of things were approached from the correct angle, order would

---

[21] Ibid., 846.
[22] Roger Lewin, *Complexity: Life at the Edge of Chaos* (New York: Macmillan, 1992), 38.

appear (S, 39), but only when the cosmos is looked at as a whole (HP, 15).

However, Wolfram's materialistic view would cause Teilhard great concern. To Wolfram, the human is merely another computational equivalent to others in the universe. He reduces both natural processes and those produced by human effort to computations,[23] disregarding what Teilhard would consider a most important part of the cosmic fabric—its inner face, the sacred depths of nature.

Recently, some complexity scientists have challenged the neo-Darwinian claim that new types of organisms arise from the interplay of genetic mutations and natural selection alone.[24] They now go one step further. They have introduced what they consider are equally important, evolutionary mechanisms—self-organization and historical accident.[25] They are trying to understand how the cell, with the help of mutation and natural selection, organizes itself into robust patterns of activity. Struck by "the extraordinary surge toward order" found in living systems,[26] Stuart Kauffman, for instance, uses these principles to explore the evolution of biological systems. He expects that his research will uncover what Lewin calls "a deep theory of order in biology."[27] To study the emergence of biological order, Kauffman is modeling the process of natural selection with an updated version of the adaptive fitness landscape.

---

[23] Wolfram, *A New Kind of Science*, 715.

[24] Emergent phenomena are regularities of behavior that somehow seem to transcend their own ingredients. For instance, the color of a chemical does not reside in the individual atoms or molecules that make it up but emerges only because of the complex interaction of one element with the other (Jack Cohen and Ian Stewart, *The Collapse of Chaos: Discovering Simplicity in a Complex World* [New York: Penguin Group, 1994], 232). Life is also an emergent property, because it is present only in the whole.

[25] Kauffman, *At Home in the Universe*, 8.

[26] Ibid., 10.

[27] Lewin, *Complexity*, 43.

When first introduced by geneticist Sewall Wright in the 1930s, the adaptive fitness landscape was simply a crude map that resembled a terrain of rolling hills where individuals assumed to be more fit were placed on the upper slopes and on the tops of the hills, and less fit individuals were placed along the lower slopes and in the valleys. Individuals near the top were more likely to survive, while those in the valleys tended to die off.[28] Wright's model depicts evolution as the struggle of a population, driven by natural selection, to climb to the top of a local fitness peak. Over the years methods for working with adaptive fitness landscapes were improved so that they were eventually able to include the interaction of species with species and with the environment and processes by which a population of homogeneous cells differentiates into an organism's diverse cell types.

When Gregor Mendel first discovered that traits are passed from one generation to the next by means of genes, he devised a simple model: Each trait is determined by a pair of genes, one from each parent, and each containing two alleles. Each allele is coded for one value of the trait, where one of these values is dominant and the other is recessive. Only when both genes contain two recessive alleles would the recessive trait definitely appear in the next generation. However, it is now clear that the traits of most organisms are determined by many genes, each with several alleles. This results in a huge number of possible combinations creating a fitness landscape of organisms with seemingly continuous variation.[29]

To explore these more intricate and realistic landscapes, biologist Stuart Kauffman and his co-workers have devised computer algorithms that generate adaptive landscapes and then search these landscapes for fitness peaks. To illustrate

---

[28] N. Eldridge and S. J. Gould "Punctuated Equilibria: An Alternative to Phyletic Gradualism," in *Models in Paleobiology*, ed. T. J. M. Schef (San Francisco: Freeman, 1972), 126.

[29] Melanie Mitchell, *Complexity: A Guided Tour* (New York: Oxford University Press, 2009), 80–82.

this method, we choose a simple adaptive landscape to represent a genome consisting of four genes, each with two alleles, that is, two values such as short/tall or pink/blue. If the value assigned to each allele is represented in this model by either 0 or 1, the following sixteen possible genotypes result: (1111), (1110), (1100), (1101), (1011), (1010), (1000), (1001), (0100), (0111), (0101), (0110), (0001), (0011), (0010), and (0000). If these genotypes are placed at the edges of a hypercube, each gene has four nearest neighbors. Each artificially generated genotype is then randomly assigned a fitness level from 1 to 16. Because the fitness contribution of the allele of one gene to the whole organism may depend in complex ways on the alleles of other genes, Kauffman includes interaction among the genes in his model. When he uses this model to explore the effect of interaction for large populations, he finds that if genes are considered independent, the resulting landscape contains a single peak making the system too ordered for creative evolution to take place. On the other hand, if each gene is considered to be strongly correlated to every other gene, the landscape is random and rugged—it exhibits many isolated local peaks and adaptation slows. Since an organism cannot find higher peaks in the immediate vicinity, adaptation stops. However, there is a transition region between the two extremes of ordered stability and chaotic instability called the edge of chaos. In this region populations are slightly unstable. As they interact with the environment, they are creative enough to evolve and form stable structures. Kauffman notes that physical processes can be transformative only when systems move from their stable environment into that far-from-equilibrium situation that borders on the turbulent.[30]

Although the term was not yet in use in his day, Teilhard knew what it meant to live at the edge of chaos. In the trenches during World War I he had experienced the terrors of war, and while serving as a stretcher bearer, he had literally looked death

---

[30] Kauffman, *At Home in the Universe*, 87.

in the face. Yet, despite feelings of horror that were always present, he also experienced feelings of freedom, unanimity, and exhilaration (HM, 168–80), feelings that are known only to those who experience the danger of the battlefront. The front served as a metaphor for the far-from-equilibrium region, "essentially relative and shifting" (D, 108), the edge of chaos that separated the traumatic events of his life from the stable. Teilhard wrote to his cousin, Marguerite, describing the evolutionary front as "the final boundary between what has already been achieved and what is striving to emerge . . . the *extreme boundary* between what one is already aware of, and what is still in process of formation" (MM, 203–4). It is a place of creativity where one experiences enough stability to maintain daily activities, but also enough dynamism to continue searching for new ways to approach life.

Like the complexity scientists, Teilhard realized that this kind of creativity results only from dealing with opposing forces: the "process of 'arrangement' which . . . produces the infinite variety . . . of ever more complex . . . atoms, molecules, living cells, etc." and "the process of 'dis-arrangement' (Entropy), which is constantly bringing arranged Energy back to its most probable . . . forms" (HM, 84). It is interesting to note that his synthesis began to take shape during his time on the battlefront.

For Teilhard, "the self-organization of the world progresses only by dint of countless attempts to grope its way" (C, 187). Like points on the fitness landscape, spiritual paths available for the mystical ascent must be carefully discerned before they are taken. Teilhard often used a landscape image to describe his spiritual journey. He pictured the mystic as

> a traveller on a fog-bound mountain-side climbing upward toward the summit bathed in light . . . placed . . . on its slopes, at a specific point defined by the present moment in the history of the world, the place of our birth and our individual vocation. And *from that starting point* . . . the task assigned to us is to climb toward

the light, passing through, so as to attain God, *a given series of created things* which are not exactly obstacles but rather foot-holds, intermediaries to be made use of. (D, 107–8)

Just as "all the roads that life tries in order to effect the synthesis . . . are not equally profitable" (W, 158), just as each evolving center "does no more than grope its way forward, one approximation following upon another" (T, 60), just as a researcher must experiment with a variety of approaches before finding one that solves the problem at hand, so the mystic must "test every barrier, try every path, plumb every abyss" (D, 70) to discern the way forward. Keeping passionate and focused is a critical component of the mystical life: "Without . . . passion for the great peaks, there would have been no ascent" (C, 222).

As Teilhard moved through the Circle of Energy, he could no longer view the cosmos as fragmented and static. It became instead dynamic and organic. Now, no longer simply consistent, the universe was alive, vibrant, filled with Divine Energy, and solidly enduring (W, 124). The heavens are in constant flux; the mineral world is ever changing; the biosphere seethes with activity. In fact, the cosmos is undergoing a cosmogenesis (HM, 25), a vast and continuing process (F, 17) of development that is slowly moving it toward greater complexity and deeper union: "Creation has never stopped. The creative act is one huge continual gesture, drawn out over the totality of time. . . . The world is constantly emerging" (W, 130). Each new discovery carried him deeper into this ocean of energy (W, 129). What had at first seemed to him "an unimaginable tangle of chances and mishaps" is actually being "directed by a power that is eminently in control of the elements that make up the universe" (S, 41).

As he viewed the organizational processes at work within the very fabric of the cosmos, its amazing potential and energy, he sensed something greater, something responsible for the order that pervades the cosmos, something that guides the cosmos as it moves toward ever greater novelty. The Divine Presence that had become so powerfully real to him in the first circle not only holds things together, as he experienced in the second circle, but is also the Divine Energy that provides the inner thrust for the cosmic becoming, the energy that facilitates Creative Union. In the third circle Divine Presence became for him Divine Energy, "the fire that consumes and the water that overthrows" (HM, 69), the impetus underlying all natural energy, guiding its every action. Divine Energy "insinuates itself everywhere and is everywhere at work" (D, 109), especially at the very heart of the cosmos. The rock whose hardness and durability had charmed him as a child lost its place as the primary object of his adoration. Now, he was "obliged to identify the extreme Solidity of things with *an extreme organic complexity*" (HM, 28).

Teilhard was only too mindful of the pain and suffering that accompany the ordinary course of life and the roadblocks that often stand in the way, even in the path of one who sincerely works for the good of the world. His service as a stretcher bearer during World War I put him in close contact with the brutality of war and face to face with death. His efforts to affect a synthesis were repeatedly rejected by the authorities of the church that he loved so deeply. His efforts to articulate a vision that would, in fact, have energized both the church and the world were discounted. For almost twenty years he lived as an exile in China, often not permitted to return to his home country, which he loved so dearly.

Yet, Teilhard was not one to wallow in misery. Putting his personal suffering into a cosmic perspective, he turned his attention to the pain and suffering that pervades the evolutionary story, a story that is rife with misfortune, struggle, disease, and death: natural disasters beset Earth on every side; predators prey on more vulnerable species; changing environmental conditions cause many species to become extinct; within the human community, war and oppression continue to rage. It is not only humans who suffer. Every part of the cosmos bears the scars of the chaos and tragedy that accompany the evolutionary process.

On the surface, the presence of evil and suffering might seem pointless. However, over the years people have tried to make sense of their pain. Many religions, steeped as they are in a static understanding of creation, have traditionally interpreted suffering as the debt that all humans must pay for an original fall. Suffering is seen as expiation for the sin of the past, a way to atone for wrongdoing and to return to a lost paradise. Many scientists, on the other hand, who are steeped in a materialist worldview, explain suffering and evil exclusively in terms of evolutionary adaptation in which promoting the survival of human genes is the primary evolutionary force.[31]

Teilhard differs with both groups. Rather than pining for a lost idyllic past, rather than blaming evil on the sins committed by our ancestors, he sees suffering and evil as the natural products of an unfinished world, the price one must pay to live, to enjoy freedom, and to grow (W, 71). In fact, the emergence of new structures is often accompanied by violent processes: simple nuclei collide violently and form more complex nuclei; supernovas explode to provide rich material for future planetary systems; volcanoes erupt and cause devastation, yet eventually the soil in the area becomes quite fertile, a blessing for future farmers. If understood properly, suffering has teleological value; it is life's warning system, causing us to reevaluate our life direction, moving us toward eventual fulfillment, deepening our sense of compassion, and requiring that we seek companionship and community along the way as we travel toward an uncertain yet promising future.[32]

Teilhard wanted to overcome suffering and evil of every kind but realized that suffering can often be unyielding. Sometimes

---

[31] John Haught, "Teilhard and the Question of Life's Suffering," in *Rediscovering Teilhard's Fire*, ed. Kathleen Duffy, SSJ (Philadelphia: St. Joseph University Press, 2010), 57.

[32] Ibid., 53–67.

it is appropriate to surrender. He found that, at those times, he needed to assume the attitude of an artist:

> An honest workman not only surrenders his calm and peace once and for all, but must learn continually to jettison the form which his labour or art or thought first took, and go in search of new forms. To pause, so as to bask in or possess results, would be a betrayal of action. Over and over again he must go beyond himself, tear himself away from himself, leaving behind him his most cherished beginnings. (D, 71)

Despite the many obstacles that Teilhard encountered during his lifetime, he found that suffering and death could no longer touch the core of his being or destroy it. His eyes instead were "set on the future" (W, 195). He often quoted the adage of geologist Pierre Termier, "Everything that happens is adorable" (LT, 183n1).

Teilhard realized that the evolutionary world is not complete. Instead, creation is ongoing, "a *work* to be carried through" (HM, 203), and he understood the need for participation. In the domain of action, he was knit together with the Divine (D, 64), able to "adhere to the creative power of God" and to "merge . . . with the very heart of God" (D, 62–63). It was by participating in this process that he could adapt to the Divine Fire at work at the heart of matter (W, 133). Teilhard perceived Divine Energy everywhere:

> at the tip of my pen, my spade, my brush, my needle—of my heart and of my thought. By pressing the stroke, the line, or the stitch, on which I am engaged, to its ultimate natural finish, I shall lay hold of that last end towards which my innermost will tends. (D, 64)

Creative activity closely coupled with the work of Divine Energy has its ecstatic side. Feelings of delight accompany this kind of action:

Those who spread their sails in the right way to the winds of the earth will always find themselves borne by a current towards the open seas. The more nobly a man wills and acts, the more avid he becomes for great and sublime aims to pursue. He will no longer be content with family, country and the remunerative aspect of his work. He will want wider organisations to create, new paths to blaze, causes to uphold, truths to discover, an ideal to cherish and defend. So, gradually, the worker no longer belongs to himself. Little by little the great breath of the universe has insinuated itself into him . . . has broadened him, raised him up, borne him on. . . . It is not himself that he is seeking, but that which is greater than he, to which he knows that he is destined. In his own view he himself no longer counts, no longer exist; he has forgotten and lost himself in the very endeavour which is making him perfect. (D, 72–73)

Teilhard realized that just as the evolutionary cosmos has, throughout its nearly fourteen billion year lifetime, been groping, straining forward to develop new forms, to find new solutions to the problems at hand, humanity too must develop this kind of creativity. He had learned much about this discernment process from nature:

The labour of seaweed as it concentrates in its tissues the substances scattered, in infinitesimal quantities, throughout the vast layers of the ocean; the industry of bees as they make honey from the juices broadcast in so many flowers—these are but pale images of the ceaseless working-over that all the forces of the universe undergo in us. (D, 60)

Before Teilhard grasped the spacetime history of the cosmos with its amazing transitions from matter to life, and from life to mind, it was difficult for him to understand the value of his work and to be motivated to act for the future.

Reading Earth's story changed this. He began to see that the universe, in response to Divine Attraction, is still being molded like clay (D, 135). Furthermore, it became clear that human action has "a universal, absolute, value. . . . Its aim is . . . to channel . . . *the whole* of the World's drive towards the Beautiful and the Good" (HM, 204). This motivated him to work in resonance with Divine Energy, to trust that his own action would be effective.

Having experienced the dynamic and unitive activity of the cosmos and "the flame of organic development . . . running through the world since the beginning of time" that gives it its consistence (HM, 138), Teilhard desired to dedicate himself to work in resonance with Divine Energy. He wanted to facilitate creative action in any way that he could and to be guided by the divine influence in which he was embedded. Work done in harmony with Divine Energy became for him a sacred duty. Because his actions were contributing to the larger project of unification going on everywhere in the cosmos, he knew that the fruit of his efforts would survive and transcend the short span of his life. This gave him comfort. He vowed: "*I shall work together with your action . . . and will do so doubly. First, to your deep inspiration . . . I shall respond by taking great care never to stifle nor distort nor waste my power to love and to do*" (D, 79). Teilhard discovered that

> purity does not lie in separation from, but in a deeper penetration into the Universe. It is to be found in the love of that unique boundless Essence which penetrates the inmost depths of all things and there, from within these depths, deeper than the mortal zone where individuals and multitudes struggle, works upon them and moulds them. Purity lies in a chaste contact with that which is "the same in all." (HM, 71–72)

He was convinced that he must steep himself in the sea of matter, bathe in its fiery water, plunge into Earth where it is deepest and most violent, struggle in its currents, and drink of its waters. Earth was the source of his life: through the world Divine Energy enveloped him, penetrated him, and created him. Because Earth had cradled him long ago in his preconscious existence, he knew that the Earth would now raise him up to God (HM, 72).

At certain times, often when he was immersed in the complexity and immobility of his rocks, Teilhard became overwhelmed by Divine Energy. He once wrote to a friend:

> Personally, I am fine. I have been sufficiently absorbed in study of the terrain not to have time to think about personal or serious things. But as I was telling you, this contact with the real does me good. And then, amid the complexity and immobility of the rocks there rise suddenly toward me "gusts of being," sudden and brief fits of awareness of the laborious unification of things, and it is no longer myself thinking, but the Earth acting. It is infinitely better. (LTF, 73)

Determined to work in consonance with Divine Energy, he no longer depended on his ego for direction (D, 70–72). His support came instead from the total awareness of what is going on in the cosmos and his place in it. He knew the true sense of freedom that all mystics who live in congruence with the will of God come to know.[33] Convinced of Divine Energy's unifying presence, he committed himself to participate in the great work of bringing all things into one and chose to risk all to carry it out. "Turning his eyes resolutely away from what was receding from him, he surrendered himself, in superabounding faith, to the wind which was sweeping the universe onwards" (HM, 74).

So many things which once had distressed or revolted him . . . seemed to him now merely ridiculous, non-existent,

---

[33] Dorothee Soelle, *The Silent Cry: Mysticism and Resistance* (Minneapolis: Fortress Press, 2001), 210, 216.

compared with the majestic reality, the flood of energy, which now revealed itself to him: omnipresent, unalterable in its truth, relentless in its development, untouchable in its serenity, maternal and unfailing in its protectiveness. (HM, 73)

It was in a spirit of deep joy that Teilhard immersed himself in this "deep-running ontological, total Current which embraced the whole Universe" (HM, 25).

5.

The Circle of Spirit

The internal face of the world comes to light and
reflects upon itself
in the very depths of our human consciousness.

—Pierre Teilhard de Chardin,
The Human Phenomenon, 29

Amazed by the physical processes at work in the cosmos
and alive with the fire of Divine Energy, Teilhard approached
the fourth circle, the Circle of Spirit. There he embarked on
the next phase of his solitary journey into the expanding and
evolving universe—this time to explore more fully its inner
face. He began by plumbing the depths of his own being,
plunging into the current that was his life so that he could
chart the development of his person from the very beginning. He wanted to see whether, and if so how, the principle
of Creative Union was operating in his own cosmic story.
Grasping one of the cosmic threads that are mapping out the
cosmic becoming and venturing through the maze of cosmic
fibers, Teilhard began his exploration. He shares this powerful moment:

And so, for the first time in my life perhaps (although
I am supposed to meditate every day!), I took the lamp

and, leaving the zone of everyday occupations and relationships where everything seems clear, I went down into
my inmost self, to the deep abyss whence I feel dimly
that my power of action emanates. But as I moved further and further away from the conventional certainties
by which social life is superficially illuminated, I became
aware that I was losing contact with myself. At each step
of the descent a new person was disclosed within me of
whose name I was no longer sure, and who no longer
obeyed me. And when I had to stop my exploration because the path faded from beneath my steps, I found a
bottomless abyss at my feet, and out of it came—arising
I know not from where—the current which I dare to call
my life. (D, 76–77)

Peering into the deep inner chasm from which his life current emerged, Teilhard found himself once again immersed
in an intricate network. At first, he "felt the distress characteristic to a particle adrift in the universe" (D, 78), lost in the
cosmic expanse. The immensity and grandeur of the universe
overwhelmed him. As he descended back through the eons
of time, the landscape became less and less familiar; patterns
came and went at random and then disappeared. Finally, near
the beginning of time, all cosmic structure dissolved into a
sea of elementary particles. Troubled, at first, by the apparent
lack of unity, Teilhard reversed his direction, exploring instead
the cosmic becoming. As he moved forward through time,
he watched elementary particles fuse into fragile streams.
Amazed by how these streams continued to coalesce, he focused on those that would eventually form his own current,
noting the way they converged. Extending "from the initial
starting-point of the cosmic processes . . . to the meeting of
my parents" (W, 228), rivulets were growing in strength and
beauty. As time progressed, they came alive—they began
cascading in torrents, swirling in eddies, pulsating with life
and with spiritual power. Teilhard could feel the energy of life
gushing from his core.

The more Teilhard explored the cosmic landscape, the more an intangible spiritual layer became apparent. The power and beauty of this spiritual energy opened his eyes to the inner face of evolution: "Everywhere in the stuff of the universe there necessarily exists an internal conscious face lining the external 'material' face habitually the only one considered by science" (HP, 26). As he allowed the beauty of the cosmos to flood his spirit, he became more and more capable of accessing matter's inner dimension, of exploring evolution's inner face (HP, 36).

Teilhard had puzzled over cosmic energy for a long time and was able to differentiate two types. From his study of the physical sciences, he was familiar with the energy needed for physical processes such as fusion, crystal formation, organic synthesis, and biosynthesis. This kind of energy links elements on the same level into somewhat rigid structures, ever working in opposition to the movement of entropy[1] and always encouraging self-organizing behavior. He called this kind of energy "tangential energy." However, he also noticed yet another type of energy, a psychic form that is responsible for evolution's forward movement. To this energy, which he called "radial energy," he attributed the emergence of new and more complex forms and particularly the critical transitions from matter to life and from life to thought.[2] Radial energy encourages matter not only to interact but also to generate novelty.[3] "The mere organic combination of a number of elements inevitably brings about the *emergence* in nature of something completely new (something 'higher')" (A, 131–32). Despite the fact that both forms of energy were present from the beginning, radial energy and its attendant spiritual power became conspicuous only gradually, bursting forth more clearly as

---

[1] Thomas M. King, *Teilhard's Mysticism of Knowing* (New York: Seabury Press, 1981), 121.

[2] To satisfy the universally accepted physical law of conservation of energy, Teilhard argues that radial energy becomes measurable only at high radial values (HP, 31).

[3] King, *Teilhard's Mysticism of Knowing*, 120–23.

life emerged on Earth. The profound symmetry that Teilhard notes between his own psychic energy and radial energy with its power to drive the evolutionary becoming, encouraged him to explore its source, to learn more about its properties, which tend to intensify as matter complexifies (HP, 30n).[4]

The prediction that entropy should already have caused Earth's heat death was quite strong in Teilhard's day and heralded a world of decline and increasing disorder.[5] The second law of thermodynamics states that a closed system will move spontaneously toward greater disorder, that is, greater entropy, and eventually run out of useful energy. This happens because heat travels naturally only from hot to cold. Once the temperature of any isolated system becomes uniform and no external energy source is available, its energy becomes useless and unable to do work. For an open system, on the other hand, energy inputs from sources outside the system continue to fuel internal processes and prevent the onset of heat death. Living things do, in fact, degrade the energy content of their environment, increasing the entropy of the system,[6] but living systems continue to thrive so long as energy inputs are large enough to counteract the effects of this degradation. On planet Earth, solar energy provides the fuel needed so that living organisms can grow and develop and thus overcome the drive toward greater entropy. Teilhard's knowledge of these thermodynamic principles reassured him that planet Earth is not on its way to imminent heat death. Instead, he viewed life on Earth as "a local counter-current, an eddy in entropy" (V, 150).

---

[4] James Salmon, SJ, "Teilhard's Science," in *Rediscovering Teilhard's Fire*, ed. Kathleen Duffy, SSJ (Philadelphia: St. Joseph's University Press, 2010), 180–84.

[5] John H. Cartwright and Brian Baker, *Science and Literature: Social Impact and Interaction* (Santa Barbara, CA: ABC-CLIO, 2005), 247.

[6] Albert Lehninger, *Principles of Biochemistry*, 2d ed. (London: Worth Publishers, 1993).

It was clear to Teilhard that, for consciousness to have evolved to its present state, "a certain mass of elementary consciousness becomes imprisoned in terrestrial matter at the beginning" (HP, 37) and . . . over time, it continued to grow stronger and more robust. Contemplating the first cells bubbling up from Earth's ocean floor, Teilhard was aware of more than the evolution of matter; he realized that he was also witnessing the evolution of spirit.

This psychic centering process became evident to Teilhard only after he had learned to look at the evolutionary phenomenon as a whole, to place the human phenomenon within the context of the total story of the Universe. In fact, he found that once the evolutionary cosmos is looked at as a whole, "as a single organic object" (S, 89), the world becomes "an interdependent mass of infinitesimal centers structurally interconnected by their conditions of origin and their development" (HP, 38). Again, it is a matter of seeing properly:

> If we wish to discern the phenomenon of spirit in its entirety, we must first educate our eyes to perceiving collective realities. Because we are ourselves individuals, life around us affects us principally on the individual scale. Atoms ourselves, we first see only other atoms. But it does not require much reflexion to discover that animate bodies are not as separate from one another as they appear. Not only are they all, by the mechanism of reproduction, related by birth. But by the very process of their development, a network of living connexions . . . never for a moment ceases to hold them in a single tissue. (HE, 95)

For Teilhard, Matter and Spirit are not only complementary aspects of a single reality; they also evolve in complementary ways: The more complex matter becomes, the more capable it is of embodying a more developed consciousness or spirit (W, 155). And as spirit deepens, the physical matrix becomes capable of greater complexity: "And here is the lightning-flash that illuminates the biosphere to its depths. . . . . Everything is in motion, everything is raising itself, organizing itself in a single direction, which is that of the greatest consciousness" (V, 72). Matter and spirit are so intimately interconnected that one has not evolved without the other. In fact, "the more intimate the union effected between more diverse elements . . . the more perfect and conscious the being that emerged" (W, 155). This process of parallel growth has culminated to date in the human who possesses a highly complex brain capable of supporting a high level of consciousness, one that is self-reflective.

The gradual emergence of consciousness so conspicuous in the evolutionary story convinced Teilhard that the Cosmos has a goal. He notes that "Spirit is the goal towards which nature's age-long labours are directed" (W, 137). In fact, "the progressive spiritualization of conscious being" assured him that the cosmos will continue to produce ever higher degrees of spirit (S, 41): "'Consciousness' . . . has in my eyes become the 'fundamental element,' the very stuff of the real . . . and the current 'towards greater consciousness' should . . . displace physically the current of 'Entropy' in its dignity as current expressing 'the universal drift'" (LLZ, 87). Just as the genomes on the evolutionary landscapes generally drift toward more fit populations, so matter experiences "a *general 'drift'* . . . *towards* spirit" (D, 110). Everything is "driven, from its beginning, by an urge toward a little more freedom, a little more power, more truth" (W, 137). Having witnessed the movement of the evolutionary process toward complexity, Teilhard was confident that "the universe, *as a whole*, cannot ever be brought to a halt or turn back in the movement which draws it towards a greater degree of freedom and consciousness" (C, 109).

Teilhard discerned qualitative laws of growth (HP, 27–28). For matter in general, there is a passive aspect to growth: "to be more [that is, to be more conscious] is to be more fully united with more." This assertion makes complexity the measure of matter's being. However, there is also a more active aspect to growth: "to be more is more fully to unite more" (S, 45).[7] The one who is fully alive then is the one who is creative and innovative, the one who relates to the other, the one who draws together persons, places, and things, as well as information and knowledge from whatever is available in the environment. Relationship and creativity are signs of fullness of being. In fact, this view expands the metaphysics of being into a metaphysics of becoming, suggesting a more dynamic definition for growth in the cosmos.[8]

The appearance of the human with a mind that can reflect on itself is a most significant event in the history of the cosmos, the result of a long process of emergence that began with the appearance of elementary matter. It represents a second phase transition. Human consciousness, due in part to the size and complexity of the human brain, is presently the most developed expression of matter's inner conscious face. The human is not merely another computational equivalent to all the others in the universe as Steven Wolfram would have it. Instead, according to Teilhard, the human has a special place in the cosmic hierarchy. At the forefront of Earth's development and on the principal axis of the universe, the human "represents the highest embryonic stage we know in the growth of spirit on Earth" (C, 106). As the embodiment of the greatest degree of consciousness and freedom achieved by evolution to date, humanity finds itself at "a naturally advantageous panoramic point" (HP, 4). The view from this point gives the evolutionary process perspective and meaning: "As soon as we look for the expression of a constant drive

---

[7] Ignatius of Loyola, the founder of the Jesuit order, encouraged his men to strive for "the more." It is little wonder, then, that Teilhard tries to define what it means to be more.

[8] James Salmon and Nicole Schmitz-Moormann, "Evolution as Revelation of a Triune God," *Teilhard Studies* 46 (Spring 2003).

towards a higher degree of spontaneity and consciousness, then the whole readily falls into position; and thought finds its natural place in this development" (HP, 38).

Teilhard focused his attention on the shape and texture of the spiritual fabric that silently, almost imperceptibly (HP, 125), is enveloping our Earth. He envisioned golden threads of spirit interwoven among crimson threads of matter, each supporting the other and holding the whole together—quanta of matter weaving a material fabric throughout spacetime; quanta of spirit weaving matter's psychic component. Like a chaotic attractor that seems to wander where it will despite the fact that it is being guided by deterministic forces, the fabric of spacetime has a shape and form that is unpredictable. Chance meetings of strands within this tangle of fibers prepare the way for the emergence of ever greater novelty.

Teilhard visualized the vast network of human consciousness surrounding Earth and called it the noosphere.[9] This spherical shell of psychic energy crowns the other spheres of Earth—the barysphere, the lithosphere, the hydrosphere, and the biosphere—and "corresponds *interiorly* to the installation of a psychic state in the very dimensions of the Earth" (HP, 95). The elements of the noosphere are like "the cells of a highly specialized organism" (HE, 131), each with its own special function. A thinking network, the noosphere is capable of self-reflection and thus of furthering its own progress (V, 73). The structure of the noosphere is akin to "a vast nervous system" (HP, 95) with "fibers and ganglions on the surface; consciousness deep within" (HP, 95), producing a collective brain with a collective memory (HP, 142). The web of social, political, and economic connections that surrounds

---

[9] Siôn Cowell defines the noosphere as "the spiritual (or thinking) layer of the world, a new biological kingdom, an organic and specific whole in process of unanimization, distinct from the biosphere" (Siôn Cowell, *Teilhard Lexicon: Understanding the Language, Terminology, and Vision of the Writing of Pierre Teilhard de Chardin* (Portland, OR: Sussex Academic Press, 2001), 131.

our globe is merely an "external indication of another far more fundamental work that is presently taking place: the inner psychical organization of the noosphere" (HE, 136). This most remarkable layer (S, 93), this "animated covering of our planet" (HE, 95), continues to multiply its internal fiber, tighten its network (F, 137), and hold these living connections in a single web.

Because it is psychic, the noosphere's energy is difficult to measure. Yet, just as a geologist can sense the violent activity deep within Earth's core with a seismometer, so a mind alert to the presence of spirit can discern the vitality and movement of the noosphere (HE, 122–23). Or just as "electrical charges distributed uniformly along a conductor" indicate the presence of an electric field, conscious beings, Teilhard claimed, are simply the local manifestations of a single spirit, the spirit of Earth (HE, 95).

The noosphere is conscious of itself and capable of collaboration, of spiritual relationship, and of sympathy, and thus of counteracting the dissolution brought on by individualization (V, 73). It is a "tenuous envelope . . . an almost insignificant film" (HE, 121), yet because of its capacity for relationship, it can overcome any innate tendency to fragment (V, 73). It is a "sphere . . . of the conscious unity of souls" (V, 63). In fact, Teilhard called it "the very Soul of the Earth" (HM, 32). The tendency of the noosphere toward a higher spiritualization continues on, "animated by a movement of its own, drawing it towards a spiritual realization of a higher order" (HE, 122). "The thinking network is gradually expanding and tightening" (HP, 135), expanding in space as it increases in spiritual depth (HE, 137). As it weaves its ever-complexifying web, the noosphere continues to increase its "incredible potential for the unexpected" (HP, 195).

The seat of consciousness is generally considered to reside in the human brain, although in former times it had been thought to reside in the heart. In any case, scientists such as Jeff Hawkins believe that "the question of intelligence is the last great terrestrial frontier of science."[10] Archeologist Steven Mithen attributes the power of the human brain to the way the brain has evolved. He likens its gradual development to that of a medieval cathedral. The simple central nave of the early cathedral is comparable to the part of the brain responsible for the kind of generalized intelligence evident in our early ancestors. As the brain complexified through processes of random mutation and natural selection, it acquired certain specialized but isolated functions, the way early cathedrals gradually acquired isolated side chapels. With time, disconnected cognitive domains emerged, each domain dedicated to a specific function. Eventually, the chapels became connected to the main nave. In the human species the once separated domains of the brain are now interconnected. This allows information to flow freely from one part of the brain to the other, giving the modern brain a kind of cognitive fluidity that makes it possible for us to learn, to remember, to predict, and to operate at a high level of abstraction. These are functions that encourage creativity.[11] Cognitive fluidity and plasticity of the nervous system are gifts that allow self-reflective consciousness to flourish in the human.[12]

Although much is known about the structure and function of its components and much has been discovered about its evolution and its ability to learn new things, the brain is still the most complex and least-well-understood organ in the human body. An overall understanding of how its component parts work together is still lacking. Today, computer scientists are attempting to understand how the human brain functions so that they can mimic its design with intelligent machines and devices. One brain function of interest is its predictive capability. With computer programs called artificial neural

---

[10] Jeff Hawkins, with Sandra Blakeslee, *On Intelligence: How a New Understanding of the Brain Will Lead to the Creation of Truly Intelligent Machines* (New York: Times Books, Henry Holt, 2004), 1.

[11] J. Wentzel Van Huyssteen, *Alone in the World? Human Uniqueness in Science and Theology* (Grand Rapids, MI: Eerdmans, 2006), 194–97.

[12] Hawkins, with Blakeslee, *On Intelligence*, 180.

networks, computer scientists are attempting to simulate the activity of the neurons in the brain. Such research is highlighting the human brain's intricacy.

The area of the human brain that is mainly responsible for intelligent decision making is the neocortex, an area composed of between fifty and one-hundred billion cells called neurons that form the brain's communication system. A typical neuron consists of a compact cell body, or soma, with wire-like structures; many short branching fibers called dendrites, which receive signals from other neurons; and a single axon, a long thin strand that splits into thousands of branches and transmits signals to other neurons. A synapse, or connection, is formed when the end of the axon of one neuron comes very close to the dendrite of another. Whenever the first neuron sends a spike of electrical activity through its axon, the synapse converts this electrical signal into a chemical signal that will either inhibit or excite activity in the dendrites of those neurons that are connected to it. The response of the secondary neurons depends on the strength of the combined input signals from the primary neurons.

In an artificial neural network, neurons or processing units are usually arranged in three rows or layers: the input layer, the hidden layer, and the output layer. Every neuron is connected to every other neuron by means of adjustable weights, which can be either positive or negative. These weights serve to simulate excitatory or inhibitory activity. The input layer of the neural network mimics the dendrites of the biological neuron; its output layer mimics the neuron's axon. The number of neurons in an artificial neural network varies from application to application, but, to date, neural networks are still considerably scaled-down models of their biological counterparts.

Before a neural network can process data or recognize patterns, it must be trained. In the learning stage an input pattern—for instance, a letter of the alphabet—is presented to the first row of neurons. As information is fed through the network, weights and threshold values are adjusted until the network is able to identify the letter correctly. Once the network is properly trained, it can be used to make predictions, that is, to identify patterns. Unlike biological neural networks, artificial neural networks generally use feedback only in the learning stage.[13] Therefore, they work best when the pattern they are trying to identify matches exactly one of the patterns they have learned to recognize in the training stage.

Unlike artificial neurons, biological neurons in the neocortex of the human brain are structured in a more complicated hierarchy, one that allows information to flow in efficient ways. A recent approach to neural networks, called auto-associative memories, attempts to imitate this phenomenon and to improve the learning process. Auto-associative memories use feedback in both the learning stage and the using stage, enabling the neural network to predict correctly even when an input pattern is distorted or partial.

Although many neuroscientists present a dualistic picture of consciousness, where the brain is a "bodily organ that allows us to think, feel, and receive input from the external world" and the mind as the thoughts and feelings themselves, the work of radiologist Andrew Newberg and the late psychiatrist Eugene D'Aquili focuses on a more holistic description.[14] From their vantage point, mind and brain are too intimately intertwined to be considered separately. They liken the mind/brain to the wave/particle of quantum mechanics. Just as a quantum phenomenon can manifest itself either as a wave or as a particle depending on the experimental apparatus used to observe the phenomenon, so thoughts and feelings appear to originate from either the brain or the mind depending on how they are observed.[15] To study brain

---

[13] Ibid., 26.

[14] Eugene d'Aquili and Andrew B. Newberg, *The Mystical Mind: Probing the Biology of Religious Experience* (Minneapolis: Fortress Press, 1999), 21–22.

[15] Ibid., 22.

activity and to determine how individual parts of the brain work together to make up our primary consciousness circuit,[16] Newberg engages in neuroimaging experiments, particularly with practiced meditators. He feels that mystical experience, arguably the greatest mystery in neuroscience, may help in understanding consciousness. In fact, scholar of comparative religion Robert K. C. Forman claims that "in mystical experiences, the content of the mind fades, sensory awareness drops out, so you are left only with pure consciousness."[17]

All mystics, whether from East or West, seem to experience a state of absolute unitary being in which they lose "all awareness of discrete limited being and of the passage of time and even experience obliteration of the self-other dichotomy." This state results in ecstatic and blissful feelings.[18] To see how the state of mystical absorption affects brain activity, Newberg places meditators in a quiet room where, with an imaging technique called SPECT (single photon emission computed tomography) and a tracer, he detects the flow of blood through the subjects' brains. The meditators are asked to quiet their minds and to signal the researcher when they reach what they consider a peak experience. On signal, each meditator is injected with a radioactive tracer, and functional images of the meditating brain are captured and compared with the initial scans. Since blood flow correlates with neuronal activity, these images indicate the parts of the brain that are active during peak mystical experience.

To date, Newberg's results indicate that meditation and contemplation actually do affect brain activity. During a peak mystical experience, activity in the prefrontal cortex, the seat of attention, is enhanced. However, the orientation association areas, which are located in the superior parietal lobe toward

---

[16] Ibid., 67.

[17] As quoted in Sharon Begley, "Religion and the Brain," *Newsweek* (May 7, 2001), 57.

[18] D'Aquili and Newberg, *The Mystical Mind*, 110–14.

the top and back of the brain and which process information about space and time as well as the orientation of the body in space, are quiet. There is also decreased activity in the amygdala and increased activity in the hippocampus, which, since it is responsible for maintaining equilibrium, inhibits neuronal flow.[19] Results such as these occur during any focusing task, but are most intense in deep meditation.

Newberg and d'Aquili have devised a model that attempts to explain what happens during times of intense concentration, including periods of deep meditation. They postulate that such activity causes the hippocampus to block certain pathways in the brain, especially the orientation areas, and to stimulate others, setting up a reverberant feedback loop.[20] This prevents the brain from forming the distinction between self and the world, creates a sense of oneness and spiritual unity, and brings on a feeling of infinite space. As time goes on, feedback intensifies this type of brain activity. Since the language centers of the brain are bypassed during a mystical experience, deep mystical states are ineffable and difficult to describe in words.

The patterns of emergence, so clear in the fossil record, led Teilhard to consider their implications for the future of humanity. Imaging the noosphere as a kind of global brain, Teilhard began to devote more of his attention to its development. He was amazed at the potential for flourishing that resides in the noosphere. From the evidence he had gleaned as a paleontologist and from his own inner experience as a human being within an evolving world, he envisioned humanity standing at the threshold of a third major critical point in Earth's history, entering a new phase of development: "Evolution is now busy elsewhere," he said, "in a richer, more complex domain, constructing spirit, with all our minds and hearts put together" (HP, 198). Like the emergence of life

---

[19] Begley, "Religion and the Brain," 57.
[20] D'Aquili and Newberg, The Mystical Mind, 112.

and the emergence of thought, the transition to a truly global consciousness would be dramatic. Such a major transition would tend to make human thought and action more coherent, directed more toward the good of the planet as a whole and to the building up of spirit.

However, Teilhard was also keenly aware of how difficult it is to extrapolate into the future, even the near future. The "ever growing predominance of . . . individual choice" as well as the huge number of physical variables involved make an accurate prediction of the future impossible (F, 236). Yet, despite these difficulties, Teilhard stressed the importance of and the need for looking ahead to discern a probable trajectory for human becoming. In fact, the human gifts of reflection, creativity, and freedom require greater responsibility for the ongoing work of the cosmos. Action of itself is not enough; action must be effective and focused on achieving this important goal (W, 137). As co-creators in the ongoing evolution of life and spirit, the future of the cosmos depends on the choices that we make, the effort that we exert, and the work that we do.

Three trends inspired Teilhard's confidence in the future: globalization, the rapid growth of technology, and the heightening of reflection (F, 237–39). In many ways Earth has become a global village: political alliances transcend national boundaries; trade agreements fuel the global market; transportation routes allow rapid transit to all parts of the world; and communication systems, such as the Internet and telecommunications satellites, enable instantaneous connections between peoples at the remotest parts of the globe. Persons from diverse cultures find themselves linked within these networks in unprecedented ways.

Teilhard attributed the rise of globalization in part to the rapid growth of world population, which continues to increase and press us closer together physically. He illustrated the phenomenon with a simple analogy from thermodynamics. When the number of gas molecules confined to a container increases, molecules exert greater pressure on the walls of the containers because more particles are hitting the walls. Likewise, when the density of a gas increases, its molecules are more likely to interact with each other because there is less empty space available for the molecules. In the same way, when the human population continues to increase dramatically, an increase in pressure and greater interaction is more likely due not only to limited space but also to limited resources. Increased pressure can effect either positive or negative outcomes. For the molecules it can cause either an enhanced chemical reaction or an explosion. Increased pressure caused by population explosion can encourage the unification process by forcing the human community to experiment with creative ways of dealing with limits and of organizing itself so that freedom of action is enhanced. On the other hand, increased pressure may lead parts of the population to become isolated and/or aggressive. All sorts of catastrophes are possible: hunger, the rapid spread of disease, class antagonisms, war over disputed land and scarce resources, and terrorism, to name just a few. These possibilities highlight the need for the human population as a whole to choose to live in a sustainable way and to become more deeply aware of the interconnectedness that we share with one another and with all of nature: "Once having reached this summit, you will realize that nothing is isolated, nothing is either small or profane, since the humblest consciousness partially includes the destinies of the universe and cannot improve itself without improving everything around it" (LTF, 33).

Having spent much of his scientific career collecting and studying primitive tools, Teilhard knew what an important breakthrough toolmaking initiated in the early development of the human. He was therefore optimistic about the promise of technology and mechanization and enthusiastically encouraged its development. As the inventive core of the noosphere, technology is an extension of the way nature improves itself, an evolutionary enterprise in which people working together participate creatively to further the cosmic becoming. Just as "life invents" (V, 72), so too the human species participates in the ongoing evolution through invention. Technology has relieved us of tedious, mechanical, and dangerous labor; has increased the scope and clarity of our understanding of the cosmos; and has allowed us to communicate in new and remarkable ways and to perform tasks never before imagined. According to Teilhard, technology should help us to *be better*, and above all, to *be more*—spiritually stronger and more conscious. Although Teilhard was quite optimistic that a technological fix for some of these problems is possible, he realized that technical breakthroughs do not happen in a day. Even while stressing the importance of growth and development, he urged care and serious discernment in the choice of technologies, so that our future will be sustainable.

Technology can also contribute to the development of a common consciousness. Since the byproducts of technological progress, increased mechanization and technical control, bring with them a decrease in the expenditure of physical labor, technology, at its best, provides more opportunity for leisure. Besides encouraging more learning through research and continued impetus to design new and appropriate technology, leisure might also offer time for contemplation and the kind of reflection on experience needed to create a better world. This could release enormous amounts of energy that would then flow into the construction and functioning of humanity's collective consciousness (F, 239).

Teilhard cited three conditions necessary to prepare humanity for a dynamic human future: sustainable structures, education directed toward the future, and love. A successful transition to a more unified society depends to a large degree on a healthy physical matrix in which social, political, and economic systems guarantee not only survival but also a decent lifestyle for all. Basic necessities such as food, clothing, and shelter, as well as physical health and hygiene, are prerequisite. The material infrastructure to support communication, to encourage participation in shared decision making, and to guarantee a fair sharing of resources is also essential. Although deep spiritual networks across our globe are not lacking, they have not yet been vigorously pursued except when there is immediate economic and political advantage.

Education that encourages the young to adopt the values needed to make a smooth transition to a life of the spirit and to a lifestyle that is sustainable will assure the moral, ethical, and spiritual health and growth of future generations. For Teilhard, education has an evolutionary function—to develop our common memory and to ensure the noosphere's continuity. Evolution is no longer simply about the transmission of genetic information. Information of all types can now be gathered, organized, stored, and transmitted so that it is available on a global scale and for future generations. Information must also be "furthered in a reflective form and in its social dimensions" (F, 36) through the transmission of a common body of knowledge that must be reworked and improved upon continually. "A passionate faith in the purpose and splendour of human aspirations . . . must be the flame that illumines . . . teaching" (F, 37), if it is to achieve its task.

Teilhard also considered ways in which the principle of Creative Union might encourage the next major critical point in Earth's evolution: the advance from thought to what he calls superlife. He began to see that at each and every level of the cosmic hierarchy, "to receive or to communicate union is to undergo the creative influence of God . . . who creates by uniting" (S, 45). For a self-conscious being, physical forces such as gravity and electromagnetism are no longer the major forces responsible for the attraction and repulsion that drive the forefront of the evolutionary becoming. At the interpersonal level it is the force of love in its many manifestations that encourages bonding. Only interpersonal bonding processes will be capable of extending evolution beyond physics, chemistry, and biology into the psychological, social, cultural, religious, and political realms, where the centering process intensifies dramatically and provides opportunities for creating community.

Teilhard's greatest challenge to the human community is his call to "the most universal, the most tremendous and the most mysterious of the cosmic forces" (HE, 32)—to the force of love. "We have reached a crossroads in human evolution," he says, "where the only road which leads forward is towards a common passion" (B, 95). For Teilhard, "it is through *sympathy*, and this alone, that the human elements in a personalized universe may hope to rise to the level of higher synthesis" (F, 123). Just as hydrogen unites to form helium without losing its identity, so the union that Teilhard envisioned "does not enslave, nor does it neutralise the individuals which it brings together. It *superpersonalises* them" (F, 124). It is only through a high degree of sympathetic interaction that humanity will be able to reach its next critical point. Because of an ever-growing world population, as well as the continual migration of peoples, humanity is being pressed together, body to body. Through research activities that are global in nature, humanity is coming together head to head. Now, Teilhard claims, we must also choose to come together heart to heart, center to center, in a love that is differentiating and personalizing. This Teilhard called the arduous condition of human progress (F, 78). For Teilhard, "*the widest form of the love of God*" (W, 65) is displayed in building up the human species.

According to Teilhard,

> we now stand at a prodigiously interesting epoch in the earth's story. Never so conscious of their individual and collective force, but never so pervaded either by dislike of the forces of injustice and horror and irremediable death, men have once more to choose before engaging in the service of evolution. "Does life which has made us what we are deserve that we should extend it further?" (V, 76)

Never before have we been so well connected, thanks to technological advances; never before have the workings of the cosmos been so clear, thanks to scientific advances; yet, never before has humanity been so vulnerable to threats of destruction—to our environment, to our social fabric, to our cultures. The linkages that we share with one another and with our environment are increasing rapidly and becoming more obvious. Damaged waterways and polluted air currents affect us all. Poverty and degradation in one social setting have global repercussions. The present global situation, well described by the term *the edge of chaos*, finds us caught between two dangerous extremes: on the one hand, capable of interfering with natural processes in a dramatically negative way, and on the other, capable of refusing to contribute at all in a positive way to the ongoing evolution. Solutions to problems such as these require a kind of cooperation and collaboration unprecedented in human history.

Much of the difficulty stems from our inability to work effectively with one another across all sorts of boundaries: ethical, racial, religious, cultural, and national. Such interpersonal and intergroup tensions are at least as old as the human species and are the result of the way humans organize themselves. Simone de Beauvoir claims that

> the category of the "Other" is as primordial as consciousness itself. In the most primitive societies, in the most ancient mythologies, one finds the expression of a duality—that of the Self and Other. . . . No group ever sets itself up as the One without at once setting up the Other over against itself.[21]

A remarkable example of a movement that challenges this duality and focuses on the unique subjectivity of the "Other" is the Outsider Art movement. This movement aims to encourage appreciation of the artwork created by artists not recognized by the official culture and who have little or no contact with the mainstream art world or art institutions. It explores unconventional ideas, extreme mental states, and fantasy worlds.

---

[21] Simone de Beauvoir, *The Second Sex*, trans. and ed. H. M. Pashley (New York: Vantage Books, 1974), xiii–xix.

Outsider Art responds to the crying need for pluralism in today's society. As art critic Kenneth Ames notes,

> If Western Society's soul is to be saved, we need to foster values that honor and empower more of humankind. We need to continually critique reigning ideas and ideologies and do whatever we can to promote authentic pluralism. We need people who can see beyond the limited and limiting horizon of the dominant culture.[22]

It is this attitude that Outsider Art hopes to engender. Art critic Roger Cardinal, who coined the term *Outsider Art* in 1972, comments on the challenges inherent in this approach: "What Outsider Art surely asks for is a wholehearted, robust response whereby we meet it with our own sensibility fully adjusted to the moral seriousness of the occasion."[23] Willingness to listen and to try to understand the depths of another is vital to any true collaboration. Learning to look more closely at art with unfamiliar themes could lead to deeper understanding of the artist's unspoken meaning: "Once we look more closely, we may discern that which in the work conveys an individuality and therefore also a vulnerability, and we may also discern that which transcends its private discourse."[24] Cardinal goes on to describe how this might happen:

> Only by entering into something approaching the creative trance . . . can one hope for a fruitful dialogue. . . . When it happens, vulnerable oneself, one will echo and honor the vulnerability of the Outsider, and discover in

---

[22] Kenneth L. Ames, "Outside Outsider Art," in *The Artist Outsider: Creativity and the Boundaries of Culture*, ed. Michael D. Hall and Eugene W. Metcalf (Washington, DC: Smithsonian Institution Press, 1994), 270.

[23] Roger Cardinal, "Towards an Outsider Aesthetic," in Hall and Metcalf, *The Artist Outsider*, 37–38.

[24] Ibid.

this reciprocity a basis of human understanding and, as a bonus, a surge of feeling which is the aesthetic experience par excellence. The concentration, dynamic momentum, and sheer expenditure of time which are necessary for Outsider Art to accede to the status of the Beautiful (or, more strictly, the aesthetically compelling) may be seen as guarantees of its authenticity. It is the radical flavor of secrecy slowly becoming openness, of individuality slowly becoming community, which guarantees aesthetic integrity, communicating an eerie beauty born of a tension between our unsettlement and our simultaneous sense of reaching back, nostalgically to a place we somehow remember.[25]

These are extremely challenging words, words that Teilhard would most likely apply to all human endeavors that deserve the name. If humanity is to build a world of peace, only deep contemplation that takes seriously the reality of the other and longs to explore the depths of the other's reality will suffice.

Participation in the Great Work of advancing the growth of the universal Spirit (W, 137) makes all human effort valuable. However, this task requires great effort: "Progress is not immediate ease, wellbeing and peace. It is not rest." Progress is also not concerned with the total conquest of suffering and evil, a task that, despite our increased technical ability, we will never be able to achieve. Rather, "progress is a *force*, and the most dangerous of forces. It is the Consciousness of all that is and all that can be" (F, 20). Only by coming to know our place in the universe and what is happening here can humanity expect to discover the way forward. Teilhard was convinced that humanity as an organic and organized whole does have a future, albeit a future that can be achieved only through struggle and hard work (F, 192–93). In fact, he sees the evolutionary advance to greater consciousness remarkably correlated to the evolutionary advance of the

---

[25] Ibid., 39.

material world: "The slope which leads to these heights is linked so closely with the one we are already climbing naturally" (D, 70).

Unfortunately, though, too few realize their potential and/ or their responsibility for building the Earth, for contributing to the ongoing evolution. Instead, people often feel lost. Caught up in their own egoism, they disengage from global concerns. Teilhard claimed that people who understand the evolutionary process will be more willing to participate consciously to enhance its present phase and to assist in developing a more coherent approach to globalization. He felt that a sense of cosmic evolution provides motivation for the immense task at hand.

> Explain to them . . . the greatness of the current of which they are part. Make them feel the immense weight of committed efforts for which they are responsible. Compel them to see themselves as conscious elements in the complete mass of beings, inheritors of a labour as old as the world, and charged with transmitting the accumulated capital to all those who are to come. Then, at the same time, you will have overcome their tendency to inertia and disorder, and shown them what they perhaps worshipped without giving it a name. (V, 77)

Some of Teilhard's dearest friends were poets or artists. This encouraged him to reflect often on the function of the arts in the forward movement of the noosphere. He named three significant functions that the arts provide to society. First of all, artists of all kinds express the deep intuition that is fermenting in society but which, as yet, cannot be articulated; second, they intellectualize that intuition, that is, they begin to formulate concepts; and finally, they are capable of directing the spiritual energy that is at the core of their primary intuition (T, 89–90).

However, Teilhard did not consider beauty and harmony to be the purview of artists alone. Like many scientists he was allured into the study of science by the beauty of the natural world. But more than that, his work was also often inspired by beauty. Beauty became for him a herald and generator of his ideas. Likewise, Albert Einstein notes how physicist Max Planck's "longing to behold . . . harmony is the source of [Planck's] inexhaustible patience and perseverance."[26] Unity and harmony energized Planck as it has motivated many scientists throughout the ages. Although it is never a sufficient criterion for a scientific theory, beauty, harmony, and unity often point the way to a fruitful theory. A sense of harmony and beauty was also a standard for Teilhard in his search for appropriate human activity. Research that is guided by this standard is a sacred duty, a duty that, if pursued, will ensure the survival of the human species and of planet Earth.

The Great Work consists in providing impetus for the transformation to greater consciousness, promoting the cultural transition through which we, as a species, are slowly moving, fostering the next major phase transition in human history. It calls us to assess our impact, to take responsibility for our actions, and to forward the cosmic project in the direction of spirit. To do otherwise is not only irresponsible, but it is dangerous. Assessing the impact of choices on the future can be difficult because it is not always easy to see their consequences. This is particularly true in an evolutionary world, where small changes can sometimes effect major change in unforeseen directions. However, signs of movement toward and away from the light can be helpful clues in discernment. Good choices bring out the best in human nature by calling forth the greatest possible degree of consciousness, freedom, and responsibility. They focus on goals that are large enough to snatch us from our pettiness, widen our vision, and help us to desire spiritual riches such as love, wisdom, and beauty. They foster effective contributions to

---

[26] Albert Einstein, *Ideas and Opinions by Albert Einstein: Based on Mein Weltbild*, ed. Carl Seelig, new trans. and rev. Sonja Bargmann (New York: Bonanza Books, 1954).

the next stage of evolution by encouraging us to take into consideration the total organic, interdependent, and interconnected nature of the cosmos as a whole; the vast diversity of forms within matter; and the mutual interaction between spirit and matter (S, 222). This "transition from the individual to the collective is the present crucial problem confronting human energy" (HE, 150). Fidelity to the vision should help us to gain mastery over anxiety-producing tasks and move us in the direction of greater creativity, more intense exuberance, and deeper love. The world can be saved only if humanity participates in its forward movement and each person "can be saved only by becoming one with the universe" (C, 128).

Teilhard was adamant that faith in the future is a fundamental condition for survival (F, 84). "Nothing is more dangerous for the future of the world . . . than . . . resignation and false realism" (F, 154). "Zest for life" (A, 231–38) and "passion for the whole" (V, 77) were hallmarks of Teilhard's adult life and also characterize the lives of those who accept the common task. The Great Work requires a great degree of maturity and development.[27] A "flame of expectation" (F, 143) for the awakening of full human potential needs to burn. Without faith in the future, we will not have the motivation and the energy to overcome obstacles to unity. Incapable of the dream, creativity will either die or become misdirected. Teilhard had "no difficulty . . . in making his own that insatiable ardour which gives the children of earth their passion for progress" (W, 137). To participate fully, he needed to develop a deep sense of self, free from the dictates of the ego. He had to learn to go beyond the rigid boundaries of his religious and national culture so that he could continue to grow,[28] and, like the cosmos, "continually develop new forms."[29]

---

[27] See Dorothee Soelle, *The Silent Cry: Mysticism and Resistance* (Minneapolis: Fortress Press, 2001), 210.

[28] Ibid., 211.

[29] Ibid., 210.

Along the fourth circle Teilhard had confronted himself intimately. Now, as he stepped ahead, beyond the fourth circle, he began to see himself and each human person as unique, exceedingly precious, not to be exchanged for anything else.[30] He was now part of humanity, part of the cosmos, part of a synthetic process. The creative, dynamic patterns emerging in the natural world convinced him that the cosmos will continue to increase in spirit, in complexity, in union, and in love, and that humanity has a dynamic future. He committed himself to action directed toward the unification of the cosmos: *"To your all-embracing providence . . . I shall respond by my care never to miss an opportunity of rising 'towards the level of spirit'"* (D, 79).

---

[30] Van Huyssteen, *Alone in the World?* 271.

6.

The Circle of Person

*The "piece of iron" of my first days has long been
    forgotten.*
*In its place it is the Consistence of the Universe, in
    the form of Omega Point,*
*that I now hold, concentrated . . . into one single
    indestructible centre,*
WHICH I CAN LOVE.

—PIERRE TEILHARD DE CHARDIN,
The Heart of Matter, 39

Immersed in both physical and spiritual energy, Teilhard
approached the fifth circle hoping to learn more about the
elusive numinous force that animates the cosmos and draws
it forward (W, 138). In the Circle of Spirit he had come to
realize the role that the energy of love is playing in humanity's transformation to a new consciousness. As he prepared
to step into the fifth circle, into the heart of the cosmos, to
search for the source of this power, he wondered what images
might inspire him.

Although Teilhard had always been attracted to devotion to the Sacred Heart of Jesus, symbol of Christ's total
self-offering to the world, the picture of Christ offering his
heart now seemed to him too defined, too fixed, too culture

bound. As he contemplated Christ's heart and pondered how this image could be universalized, the figure of Christ and the world began to melt before his eyes into a single vibrant surface (HU, 42–43). Surrounded by a cosmic tapestry of intricately woven threads, Christ's face shone with exquisite beauty. Trails of phosphorescence gushed forth and radiated outward toward infinity. *"The entire universe was vibrant!"* (HU, 43); the cosmos had acquired a nervous system, a circulatory system, a heart. Teilhard was consumed by the fire streaming from this universal center and resolved to go deeper (HU, 44–45).

As he stepped into the fifth circle, suddenly, a shadow appeared and the figure of Sophia[1] emerged from the mists. She was radiant; her facial expression comforting. Teilhard recognized her as "the beauty running through the world, to make it associate in groups: the ideal held up before the world to make it ascend" (W, 192). From the beginning she was infused "into the initial multiple as a force of condensation and concentration." It is through her power, the power of love, that all things come together. Hidden within the very heart of

---

[1] Many of the phrases in the next few paragraphs are taken from the essay "The Eternal Feminine" (W, 191–202). In this essay Teilhard connects the Eternal Feminine to Wisdom in Ecclesiastes 24:14. See also Thomas Merton's poem "Hagia Sophia," in Thomas Merton, *Hagia Sophia* (Lexington, KY: Stamperio del Santuccio, 1962). In a conference paper Heather Eaton critiques Teilhard's use of the feminine to name attributes of God that have been excluded because of their classical connection with the feminine. This division is problematic to feminists who are trying to deconstruct this interpretation of gender. According to Eaton, what Teilhard is trying to do here is to reclaim "the validity, necessity, indeed evolutionary significance of the traits, attributes, effectiveness, aesthetics, and even epistemologies surrounding the notions or experiences of the human realities considered to be 'feminine'" (Heather Eaton, "Teilhard and Feminist Consciousness," paper presented at the Shared Legacy of Teilhard and Whitehead Conference, Claremont, February 24–26, 2005). For an alternative way of imaging Sophia's role in the cosmic becoming, see Kathleen Duffy, "Sophia: Catalyst of Creative Union and Divine Love," in *From Teilhard to Omega*, ed. Ilia Delio (Maryknoll, NY: Orbis Books, 2014).

matter, she "bestirred the original mass, almost without form
. . . and instilled even into the atoms . . . a vague but obstinate
yearning to emerge from the solitude of their nothingness."
She is "the bond that thus held together the foundations of
the universe" (W, 192–93), and she continually draws Earth
into "passionate union" with the Divine (W, 200). She is the
"magnetic force of the universal presence and the ceaseless
ripple of its smile" (W, 195), "the radiance by which all this
is aroused and within which it is vibrant" (W, 194). With the
aid of her elusive and never-ending allurements, she knits
together the fibers of spirit (W, 201–2). She is the raiment
who is forming as she is being formed, continually creating
the mystical milieu in which the forces of love encourage all
things to become one.

As life emerged and matter became capable of a richer,
deeper, and more spiritualized union, her charms increased;
she became more individualized and differentiated (W, 193).
The radiance of her countenance becomes brighter still when
it shines out from the eyes of each human face. Although her
approach can sometimes be unsettling and the violence of the
forces unleashed at her approach can stir up strong emotions
(W, 194), the purity of her love is reassuring.

The tenderness of her compassion and her holy charm (W,
200) aroused Teilhard's passion for the Divine (W, 198) and
sensitized his heart. He was enthralled with "the beauty of
spirit as it rises up adorned with all the riches of the earth"
(HM, 72), as it flows into the heart of the cosmos, toward
its very center (W, 195). He yearned to take hold of her, yet
whenever he tried, he found that she eluded his grasp (W,
195; D, 113). With great alacrity, he followed her lead as she
guided him through the "luminous mist hanging over the
abyss" (W, 200) and propelled him toward the heights into
freedom (W, 197).

In this fifth circle, the Circle of Person, a transformation
began to take place in Teilhard's very perception of being.
He "acquired a new sense, *the sense of a new quality . . . a
new dimension*" (D, 129). He became more fully aware of

the nature of the spiritual power of matter and the Divine Presence that impregnates, organizes, sustains, and energizes all things. All of his senses were affected—his sensations, his feelings, his thoughts "became more fragrant, more coloured, more intense" (D, 129). The vague note, the fragrance, and the sunbeam—those things that had so often captivated his heart—began to define themselves (D, 129). His original "vague intuition of universal unity has become a rational and well-defined awareness of a presence" (C, 117), the presence of a radiant center that has all along been alluring the cosmos into deeper and deeper union. He noted that the cosmos, which had at first seemed like a blind and feral immensity, was becoming expressive and personal. It was taking on the contours of a body and a face (HM, 124).

Up ahead, the person of Christ was coming into view. More profound than any human beauty (W, 131), his presence became "as *immediate* and all-embracing as Life" (HM, 212). The charm of his person, the tenderness of his glance (W, 131), the embrace of his "more than human arms" (D, 137), the gentle touch of his "two marvelous hands" (D, 78), hands that by the slightest pressure are capable of shaping the cosmos as if it were as pliable as clay (D, 135)—all of these attracted Teilhard to him. The warmth of his person, the radiance of his countenance, the attractive power of his soul (HM, 74) drew Teilhard so profoundly that he longed to be possessed. All at once the universe was "ablaze with the fire of divine love, suffused with the elements of a presence which beckons, summons and embraces" all of humanity,[2] and Teilhard found himself living "steeped in its burning layers" (D, 112).

As he opened the scriptures and reread the letters of Saint Paul, he was confronted with two tides of consciousness (HM, 82–83), and he began to understand more clearly Christ's evolutionary role. In "an explosion of dazzling flashes" (HM,

---

[2] Ursula King, *Spirit of Fire: The Life and Vision of Teilhard de Chardin* (Maryknoll, NY: Orbis Books, 1996), 22–23.

50), Cosmic Convergence coupled with Christic Emergence and became two phases of a single evolutionary movement. The implosion caused by the coincidence of Christ with the Omega of the Universe released "a light so intense that it transfigured . . . the very depths of the World" (HM, 82–83). All of the knowledge and love that Teilhard had for the universe was suddenly transformed into knowledge and love for the God who is embedded within every fragment of matter (HM, 200). What Teilhard had been missing all along became clear: At the apex of creation, the Universal Christ fills the cosmos. Christ is not simply the pole of consistence for the universe; he is also its prime mover (A, 147), the driving force for the complexification process, and the "ultimate psychic centre of universal concentration" (T, 199) to which all things are attracted. The universe then "is fundamentally directed by a power that is eminently in control of the elements that make up the universe" (S, 41). Christ dwells at the very heart of matter, permanently knitting together as well as being knit together with all of creation (D, 64): "Every process of material growth in the universe is ultimately directed towards spirit, and every process of spiritual growth towards Christ" (S, 68). Never coercing, always alluring, Christ acts from the future to encourage the forward movement that is occurring within the fabric of spacetime. "Only Christ, [in whom all things hold together], is capable of animating and guiding the newly sensed progress of the universe" (S, 117). Only Christ can draw all things together. Teilhard was comforted by "the calm and powerful radiance engendered by the synthesis of all the elements of the world" in Christ (D, 130). His heart was being drawn into the very heart of God.

Once Teilhard saw Christ's face "shine from within all the forces of the earth and so become visible" (HM, 131), once he realized that it was Christ's alluring presence that was drawing him into the heart of matter, he was no longer conflicted about his love for Earth. He had seen Christ, touched Christ, and heard Christ's voice. Now he knew that he would continue to have access to Christ in this way. Because the world is becoming Christ's body, Teilhard was able to love the universe as Person. At long last, "the God of Spirit" was woven together with "the Crimson of Matter" and appeared to him as "the Incandescence of Some One" (HM, 50). He longed to surrender, to allow himself to be totally grasped by Christ, whom he was encountering at the heart of matter. He exclaimed:

> Now the earth can certainly clasp me in her giant arms. She can swell me with her life, or take me back into her dust. She can deck herself out for me with every charm, with every horror, with every mystery. She can intoxicate me with her perfume of tangibility and unity. She can cast me to my knees in expectation of what is maturing in her breast. But her enchantments can no longer do me harm, since she has become for me, over and above herself, the body of him who is and of him who is coming. (D, 155)

In the Circle of Person, Teilhard's mysticism became grounded and his synthesis complete. He was confident that the universe will not only continue to complexify, but that it will also become more centered, that the body of Christ will continue to form until it is finally consummated at the end of time when all things will be one in Christ. When humanity finally transcends itself in Christ, it will inevitably find itself personally immortalized (C, 116), and "God will be all in all" (1 Cor 15:28).

Teilhard was overcome by the need to adore. He knew that this means to "lose oneself in the unfathomable, to plunge into the inexhaustible, to find peace in the incorruptible, to be absorbed in immensity, to offer oneself to the fire . . . to give of one's deepest to that whose depth has no end" (D, 127–28). He called together in spirit the vast ocean of living humanity to join him in this act of adoration (HM, 120)—all those persons who were near and dear to him, all those whom he hardly knew, and the billions of people whom he had never met. He knew that "the only human embrace capable of worthily enfolding the divine is that of all men opening their arms to call down and welcome the Fire. The only subject ultimately capable of mystical transfiguration is the whole group of mankind forming a single body and a single soul in charity" (D, 144).

The whole Earth became Teilhard's altar, the depths of his soul, his paten and chalice (HM, 119–20). Into his arms he gathered all that would grow, flower, and ripen during the day, as well as all that would corrode, wither, and be cut down; all that the evolutionary process would create, and all that would be lost through the process of entropy.[3] This was his sacrifice, gathered into his heart (HM, 122) and offered in the name of the whole cosmos. He prayed that Christ would plunge his powerful yet gentle hands into the depths of the universe, that he would breathe a soul into the newly formed fragile film of matter that would freshly clothe the world that day, to "remould it, rectify it, recast it" (HM, 122) so that every life force would be transformed into Christ's flesh and every death force would be transformed into his blood (HM, 123). Stretching his hands over these gifts, Teilhard called down the Fire (HM, 121), the Fire that has been molding and energizing the cosmos since the beginning, the Power, loving and intelligent, whose Word is capable of mastering and molding the world of matter (HM, 121). Silently and without any visible tremor, at the touch of Christ's word, "the immense host which is the universe is made flesh" (HM, 123), and Christ becomes for Teilhard the face of a world that has burst into flame.

No longer was he content simply to contemplate the Fire. He realized that he must consent to the communion (HM, 127). Stretching out his hand unhesitatingly to take the fiery bread, he gratefully accepted the life-giving forces that delighted his heart. Taking the chalice, and gazing into the

---

[3] See Thomas M. King, SJ, *Teilhard's Mass: Approaches to "The Mass on the World"* (New York: Paulist Press, 2005), 97.

unknowable future, he surrendered himself to those forces that would tear him away painfully from himself "to drive him into danger, into laborious undertakings, into a constant renewal of ideas, into an austere detachment" (HM, 128), to processes of enfeeblement, of aging, and of death (HM, 130). The Cosmic Christ had allured Teilhard into action on behalf of the final goal, guaranteeing that what is best in him should pass, there to remain forever, into one who is greater and finer than he (C, 115–16). Filled with impassioned love for Christ, he wrote, "My God, I deliver myself up with utter abandon to those fearful forces of dissolution which, I blindly believe, will this day cause my narrow ego to be replaced by your divine presence" (HM, 130). "Drawn to follow the road of fire" (HM, 74), he dedicated himself body and soul to the ongoing work needed to transform the cosmos to a new level of consciousness and of love (F, 24–25).

7.

A Spiral Journey

I am a child of Earth before being a child of God.
I only can grasp the Divine through the Cosmic.
You will never understand if you do not see that.

—Pierre Teilhard de Chardin,
Lettres à Jeanne Mortier, 58–59

As Teilhard traveled along his spiral path advancing from one circle to the next, always searching for consistency, he developed a new and more profound understanding of the mystery of the Incarnation. He began to image Christ, the Word incarnate, at the beginning of time, plunging into matter, descending into its deepest depths, penetrating to its very heart (D, 61–62) to be present to all things at all times and to hold all things together. But just as parallel rays reflecting from a spherical mirror converge at the mirror's focal point, so Christ, who is totally rooted in matter, also reappears up ahead in the future, at the focal point of the creative project, where all things will finally become one. Like Paul, who in his letter to the Romans pictures creation groaning as it awaits Christ's coming (Rom 8:22–23), Teilhard images creation groping its way as it gradually advances from inert matter, to life, to thought, and as it now struggles toward ultra-personhood.

Viewing the Incarnation through the double lens of scripture[1] and evolution, Teilhard came to recognize the Cosmic Christ as both immanent and transcendent. Immersed within the emerging universe, Christ guides the cosmos as it ascends from one critical point to another on its path toward integration (C, 75); up ahead in the future Christ encourages the cosmos to overcome its inherent resistance to unification.

Immersion and emergence (D, 110) are two phases of a single divine action that empowers the world's becoming. As a consequence of Christ's immersion, the world is filled with Divine Energy and is thus a true sacrament of Divine Presence; as a consequence of Christ's emergence, the world is continually being created, allured toward higher levels of convergence by the personalizing and unifying presence of Omega, the Cosmic Christ.

In the fullness of time, when Christ, the incarnate presence of God, appeared in human form, allowing himself to be seen and touched for a brief moment, he reenacted this sacred double gesture in two ways. As a prelude to his public ministry, Jesus plunged into the waters of the Jordan River to be baptized into matter. In this symbolic act he expressed his desire to become one with all of Earth, to bless Earth's creative forces, and to remain with and suffer with creation. After immersing himself in the bowels of Earth, he reached up to the heavens (S, 64) and, with the water still running off his body, once again elevated, blessed, and energized the whole world (D, 110). At the end of his public life, in a final dramatic reenactment and after a brutal death on Calvary, Jesus was buried in the bowels of Earth only to rise again on the third day and to ascend into the heavens. The cross of Calvary has thus become a sign of Christ's continual willingness to plunge into the fire, to engage in the purifying battle, not

---

[1] "When it says, 'He ascended,' what does it mean but that he had also descended into the lower parts of the earth? He who descended is the same one who ascended far above all the heavens, so that he might fill all things" (Eph 4:9–10).

only to expiate sin, but still more to surmount and conquer evil (C, 85). By rising from the dead, the Christ of the Gospels became the Cosmic Christ, the one who has ascended into the future and who invites all creation into unity of spirit.

The double movement of immersion and emergence, which is the hallmark of the Incarnation, is also the pattern that characterizes Teilhard's life. Along each branch of the spiral he confronted a new question and emerged with a new insight. His concern for the fragility of matter and his quest for consistence plunged him into Earth where it is most durable and most dense. Surrounded by the beauty and creativity of the natural world, he soon became aware of Earth's sacramental nature. Throughout his life he continued to immerse himself in Earth's beauty. Always "it was the world that I was in love with" (HM, 131). He emerged with an ever-deepening sense of the spiritual power diffused throughout matter, knowing that everything, no matter how insignificant, is imbued with this energizing Presence (D, 109).

Teilhard's growing knowledge of science only fueled his natural devotion to rock. As he became more acquainted with the methods of science during his teen years, his questions also became more sophisticated. Still concerned with the fragility of living things, he looked for the universal in the solid state. To search for the ultimate glue that holds things together, he once again immersed himself in Earth, this time looking for physical causes such as gravity to explain the consistence that he found in nature. As a paleontologist and geologist, he continued to dig deep into Earth's crust to discover remnants from the past and to understand Earth's formation. Intimate contact with the biosphere fed his mystical longing. He emerged from his excavations not only with fresh ways to model Earth's texture, structure, and history, but also with a deeper "*sense of the earth*" (C, 126) and a more profound encounter with the Divine Presence.

During his early formation as a Jesuit, Teilhard's natural tendency to introversion inclined him to want to immerse himself in matter, to become totally passive, and to lose himself in the cosmos (HM, 24). However, his encounter with the theory of evolution during his theological studies in England thrust him instead out into the cosmos and saved him both from the danger of remaining stuck in collecting and classifying rock and from his desire to merge with matter. His interest in the evolutionary process coupled with his interest in physics plunged him more deeply into the heart of matter and back to the beginning of time. He emerged from this journey with a profound sense of Earth's sacred evolutionary story.

Teilhard's years in the trenches during World War I helped him to face the fragility of the natural world. Experiencing the planet at its most vulnerable plunged him into that "tumultuous human mass" called humanity (HM, 188). On the battle front he was exposed to the best and worst of the human spirit. In his interactions with the soldiers in his company he came into contact with a small but diverse segment of humanity that was demonstrating its potential for unity of purpose and oneness of spirit. This helped him to envision a world in which the energy and solidarity he was experiencing on the front would one day be used, not for war, but for the advancement of human consciousness, for the creation of a world where human energy would be expended to unify rather than to divide. He emerged with a renewed sense of the beauty of the human person. His interest was no longer focused on the past. Instead, he says, "I am a pilgrim of the future on my way back from a journey made entirely in the past" (LT, 101). Now, it was the future of humanity that would interest him. He wanted to know what humanity is becoming and what, if anything, will hold it together. He wanted to discover mechanisms that will eventually drive humanity toward the critical point that will spark greater consciousness. To accomplish this task, Teilhard plunged into the Great Work, the work that humanity must accomplish to drive creation toward the fullness of being. He committed himself to becoming an actor in the evolutionary process (MM, 26) and began inviting others to see what he could see and to practice a mysticism that encourages and supports this kind of activity. In fact, Teilhard rejected a mysticism that neither accepts responsibility for the ongoing creation nor makes full use of the power of the human to love and to act. He bemoaned the fact that, for many, mysticism seems an escape from the world. Rather, Teilhard's approach to mysticism provides a solid motivation for work that is in harmony with the goals of the Cosmic Christ, who is embedded within the cosmos and is thus linked both physically and spiritually to human effort (HM, 212).

Teilhard's circle of friends and acquaintances expanded as he collaborated with the international scientific community, traveled to research sites, and lived in a variety of cultural settings. The diversity of his experiences helped him to envision the shape of a world where cooperation would prevail over competition. Aware of the noosphere, that halo of thinking energy that surrounds Earth's biosphere, he tried to imagine how the growing presence of the ever-expanding Spirit of Earth would help to mitigate the divisions among peoples often caused by physical distance from the other and by ignorance and thus by intolerance of cultural differences.

As a microcosm of humanity's transformation to a common consciousness, Teilhard's spiritual ascent was not easy. At this stage of his journey he began to experience the kinds of hazards that befall anyone who, like Christ, lives a life for others. He found himself on a road that "is not so different from the royal road of the Cross" (D, 71). Forces assailed him from all sides. Some caressed him, penetrated him, and ordered his being; others rent, shattered, and disorganized him (W, 131). Particularly during his China years, "the arms of the Cross . . . will begin to dominate the scene more widely" (D, 71). He came to know in a graphic way that "there are no summits without abysses" (HP, 206). Perhaps his inability to obtain permission to publish his religious writings caused him the most acute pain. Yet, he never abandoned his mystical path and never failed to answer what he considered a divine call. He knew that, like Christ, he would have to immerse himself in the sufferings of the world. He would have to plunge "into the world . . . to share in things and then to carry them along with him" (T, 73). Rather than swoon in the shadow of the cross, Teilhard continued to climb in its light (D, 104). Despite the pain of rejection he continued to write with the hope that one day his vision would take hold. Although in later life he was tortured by bouts of depression, his faith remained strong. The cross became, for Teilhard, a symbol that coupled humanity's struggle to overcome evil and pain with Christ's struggle to draw all things into a final unification. This understanding of the Incarnation continued to console him throughout his life. As he wrote to his brother Joseph on the occasion of the death of their sister Marguerite, "The only way of making life bearable . . . is to love and adore that which, beneath everything, animates and directs it" (LT, 227). Such optimism would have been foolish were it not for Teilhard's faith in the Cosmic Christ.

Having plumbed the depths of the human spirit, what Raimon Panikkar calls "the unbridgeable abyss of the 'I',"[2] Teilhard had reached "the heart of the cosmic Sphere, the mysterious double point where the Multiple . . . is reflected upon itself and so emerges from within into a Transcendent" (HM, 49). He knew that he was no longer capable of loving and surrendering to anything less than a person. In fact, captured by the beauty of the person of Christ at the heart of a glowing universe and by the Divine Presence radiating from the depths of blazing matter, he became convinced that the universe is evolving into a Person whom he could love.

In the act of immersing himself in the cosmos and of falling in love with the God of evolution, Teilhard became capable of uniting himself with both God and Earth in a single double movement.[3] The transcendent God who is "up above" and

---

[2] Raimon Panikkar, *Christophany: The Fullness of Man* (Maryknoll, NY: Orbis Books, 2004), 154.

[3] Dorothee Soelle, *The Silent Cry: Mysticism and Resistance* (Minneapolis: Fortress Press, 2001), 212.

was so present to him during his childhood days and the immanent God who is embedded in Earth and was so present to him in his young adulthood finally merged into a God who is up ahead. In "a flash of extraordinary brilliance" (HM, 83), "the Heart of the universalizing Christ coincided with the heart of amorized Matter" (HM, 49), and Teilhard's strong sense of God's immanence became linked with a deep sense of God's transcendence. Now that he was able to see the Divine Person of Christ shining "forth from within all the forces of earth" (HM, 131), he could surrender himself wholeheartedly.

Despite the strength of his experience of Christ's presence, Teilhard's faith did not protect him from doubt: "As much as anyone, I imagine, I walk in the shadows of faith" (C, 131). At times, he was plagued with uncertainty and with suggestions that he might be mistaken. In a 1934 essay he asserts: "I feel no special assurance of the existence of Christ. Believing is not seeing" (C, 131). At other times he experienced periods of deep loneliness. So few seemed to see what he was able to see.

Yet Teilhard accepted doubt as part of the evolutionary picture: "Our doubts, like our misfortunes, are the price we have to pay for the fulfilment of the universe, and the very condition of that fulfilment" (C, 132). He was convinced that living a life of faith is far superior to living a life of disbelief:

> If we do not believe, the waves engulf us, the winds blow, nourishment fails, sickness lays us low or kills us, the divine power is impotent or remote. If, on the other hand, we believe, the waters are welcoming and sweet, the bread is multiplied, our eyes open, the dead rise again, the power of God is, as it were, drawn from him by force and spreads throughout all nature. (D, 135)

Whenever "the shadows of faith" (C, 131) overtook him, Teilhard was comforted by the coherence, integrity, and power of his synthesis. "I am prepared to press on to the end along a road in which each step makes me more certain, towards horizons that are ever more shrouded in mist" (C, 132).

Teilhard was never content with dualistic thinking, ever balancing the rational and the numinous, the reasonable and the aesthetic, the scientific and the spiritual. He regretted the perceived dissonance between matter and spirit, between a life of prayer and a life of action, between an evolutionary future and a future that depends on a creator God. Unwilling to settle for easy solutions, he struggled with apparent contradictions until they became one. When faced with a paradox, especially one that involved faith and science, he never reduced it to an intellectual puzzle. Instead, he first descended into the deepest part of his self and there searched his personal convictions to discover the inevitable initial faith to which he could truly commit himself. Once he was convinced of the validity of his core intuition, he let what seemed conflicting influences "full freedom to react upon one another deep within" until a resolution became clear (C, 97). He waited patiently for his subjective world and his objective world to reveal a single truth. In time, "a common substratum of aspirations and illuminations" (C, 97) would emerge. Whenever his inner experience, his desires, and his dreams coincided with the direction of nature's evolutionary path, he trusted his insight and experienced what he called a complete act of knowing—"in the very act of scientifically achieving, he knew God."[4]

Teilhard's approach to mysticism was holistic. He knew that the intimate interaction of scientific observation and imaginative intuition is vital for anyone who sets out to discover the essence of the natural world.[5] Just as science alone can never plumb the inner depths of nature, so a mysticism

---

[4] Thomas M. King, *Teilhard's Mysticism of Knowing* (New York: The Seabury Press, 1981), vii.

[5] Richard Tarnas, *The Passion of the Western Mind: Understanding the Ideas That Have Shaped Our World View* (New York: Harmony Books, 1991), 378.

that is ignorant of the dynamics of the physical world can never truly know God. He hoped that one day the sciences would treat all facets of reality, that they would allow for the action of all sorts of forces: physical forces that determine interactions in matter, psychological forces that influence human interactions, as well as the super-personal Force at the heart of matter that attracts all things into ultimate unity.

At its foundation Teilhard's is a mysticism of hope, a mysticism that sustained and empowered all that he did and freed him to be what he was called to be. Nature's response to the evolutionary impulse gave him confidence in God's action in the world. The story of the universal becoming encouraged him to trust and always led him to a larger world, to a more committed stance. He knew the importance of keeping "the flame of desire ever alive in the world" (D, 151), of allowing his expectation of humanity's future to become incarnate. He sensed that the turmoil in the world was simply a sign that humanity is experiencing a major transition:

> Let us look at the earth around us. What is happening under our eyes within the mass of peoples? What is the cause of this disorder in society, this uneasy agitation, these swelling waves, these whirling and mingling currents and these turbulent and formidable new impulses? Mankind is visibly passing through a crisis of growth. Mankind is becoming dimly aware of its shortcoming and its capacities. . . . It sees the universe growing luminous like the horizon just before sunrise. It has a sense of premonition and of expectation. (D, 153)

Like the universe, Teilhard's mystical insights unfolded slowly and dramatically. As his scientific journey into the cosmos spiraled outward, his mystical journey to the heart of matter spiraled inward along those five circular paths that continued to nourish and sustain him throughout his life.

Each branch of the spiral brought him into contact with new questions, questions that arose from life experience. He paid close attention to his questions; he cared about them. They stimulated both his mind and his heart; they kept him focused and alert. Each time his knowledge of the physical world expanded, he found it necessary to reshape his understanding of the transcendent and to adjust his spirituality to the shape of the universe that was being revealed to him. He discovered that "truth . . . can be preserved only by being continually enlarged" (W, 140). By engaging questions that were so intimate and by remaining faithful to his inner voice, he unearthed hidden mystical treasures (T, 16) as well as insights that have universal appeal.

In the end, nothing was lost. Everything of value found a place in his unique synthesis. Everything held together in the light of the Cosmic Christ. Each insight represented a spiritual advance that led finally to a tangible awareness of the Divine Grasp (HM, 48). Teilhard's inner music sustained him, his love for Earth nurtured him, his interactions with others supported him, and his love for God compelled him to remain faithful. It was fidelity to his questions that made it possible for him, near the end of his life, to say to his fellow Jesuit and good friend Pierre Leroy, "I really feel that now I'm always living in God's presence."[6]

---

[6] Mary Lukas and Ellen Lukas, *Teilhard* (Garden City, NY: Doubleday, 1977), 339.

Bibliography

Ames, Kenneth L. "Outside Outsider Art." In *The Artist Outsider: Creativity and the Boundaries of Culture*, edited by Michael D. Hall and Eugene W. Metcalf. Washington, DC: Smithsonian Institution Press, 1994.

Barenboim, Daniel. *Music Quickens Time*. Brooklyn, NY: Verso, 2008.

Bartusiak, Marcia. *Einstein's Unfinished Symphony: Listening to the Sounds of Spacetime*. Washington, DC: Joseph Henry Press, 2000.

Begley, Sharon. "Religion and the Brain." *Newsweek* (May 7, 2001): 51–57.

Bernstein, Leonard. *The Joy of Music*. New York: Simon and Schuster, 1959.

Cardinal, Roger. "Towards an Outsider Aesthetic." In *The Artist Outsider: Creativity and the Boundaries of Culture*, edited by Michael D. Hall and Eugene W. Metcalf. Washington, DC: Smithsonian Institution Press, 1994.

Cartwright, John H., and Brian Baker. *Science and Literature: Social Impact and Interaction*. Santa Barbara, CA: ABC-CLIO, 2005.

Cohen, Jack, and Ian Stewart. *The Collapse of Chaos: Discovering Simplicity in a Complex World*. New York: Penguin Group, 1994.

Cowell, Sion. *The Teilhard Lexicon: Understanding the Language, Terminology and Vision of the Writings of Pierre Teilhard de Chardin*. Portland, OR: Sussex Academic Press, 2001.

Cuénot, Claude. *Teilhard de Chardin: A Biographical Study*. Translated by V. Colimore. London: Burns and Oates, 1965.

d'Aquili, Eugene, and Andrew B. Newberg. *The Mystical Mind: Probing the Biology of Religious Experience*. Minneapolis: Fortress Press, 1999.

de Beauvoir, Simone. *The Second Sex.* Translated and edited by H. M. Pashley. New York: Vantage Books, 1974.

Delio, Ilia. *Christ in Evolution.* Maryknoll, NY: Orbis Books, 2008.

Duffy, Kathleen. "The Cellular Automaton and the Cosmic Tapestry: Wolfram and Teilhard Model the Universe." *Teilhard Perspectives* 37, no. 2 (Fall 2004): 5–9.

———. "Sophia: Catalyst of Creative Union and Divine Love." In *From Teilhard to Omega,* edited by Ilia Delio. Maryknoll, NY: Orbis Books, 2014.

———. "The Texture of the Evolutionary Cosmos: Matter and Spirit in Teilhard de Chardin." In *Teilhard in the Twenty-First Century: The Emerging Spirit of the Earth,* edited by Arthur Fabel and Donald St. John. Maryknoll, NY: Orbis Books, 2003.

———. "The Texture of the Evolutionary Cosmos: Matter and Spirit in Teilhard de Chardin." *Teilhard Studies* 43 (Fall 2001).

Eaton, Heather. "Teilhard and Feminist Consciousness." Working paper, The Shared Legacy of Teilhard and Whitehead Conference, Claremont, CA, February 24–26, 2005.

Einstein, Albert. *Ideas and Opinions.* Based on *Mein Weltbild.* Edited by Carl Seelig. New translations and revisions by Sonja Bargmann. New York: Bonanza Books, 1954.

Eldridge, N., and S. J. Gould. "Punctuated Equilibria: An Alternative to Phyletic Gradualism." In *Models in Paleobiology,* edited by T. J. M. Schef. San Francisco: Freeman, 1972.

Ferris, Timothy. *The Whole Shebang: A State-of-the-Universe(s) Report.* New York: Simon and Schuster, 1997.

Frye, Marilyn. *The Politics of Reality.* New York: Crossing Press, 1983.

Gleick, James. *Chaos: Making a New Science.* New York: Viking Penguin, 1987.

Goethe, Johann Wolfgang von. *Goethe's Werke: Hamburger Ausgabe,* vol. 13, 5th ed. Hamburg: Christian Wegner, 1966.

Goodwin, Brian. *How the Leopard Changed Its Spots: The Evolution of Complexity.* New York: Simon and Schuster, 1994.

Greene, Brian. *The Elegant Universe: Superstrings, Hidden Dimensions, and the Quest for the Ultimate Theory.* New York: Vintage Books, 1999.

Grim, John. "Teilhard's Evolutionary Vision." In *Rediscovering Teilhard's Fire*, edited by Kathleen Duffy, SSJ. Philadelphia: St. Joseph's University Press, 2010.

Haught, John F. "Teilhard and the Question of Life's Suffering." In *Rediscovering Teilhard's Fire*, edited by Kathleen Duffy, SSJ. Philadelphia: St. Joseph's University Press, 2010.

Hawkins, Jeff, with Sandra Blakeslee. *On Intelligence: How a New Understanding of the Brain Will Lead to the Creation of Truly Intelligent Machines.* New York: Times Books, Henry Holt, 2004.

Jourdain, Robert. *Music, the Brain, and Ecstasy: How Music Captures Our Imagination.* New York: William Morrow, 1997.

Kauffman, Stuart. *At Home in the Universe: The Search for the Laws of Self-Organization and Complexity.* New York: Oxford University Press, 1995.

King, Thomas M. "Teilhard, Beauty, and the Arts." In *Rediscovering Teilhard's Fire*, edited by Kathleen Duffy, SSJ. Philadelphia: St. Joseph's University Press, 2010.

———. *Teilhard's Mass: Approaches to "The Mass on the World."* New York: Paulist Press, 2005.

———. *Teilhard's Mysticism of Knowing.* New York: Seabury Press, 1981.

King, Ursula. *Spirit of Fire: The Life and Vision of Teilhard de Chardin.* Maryknoll, NY: Orbis Books, 1996.

———. *Pierre Teilhard de Chardin: Writings Selected with an Introduction by Ursula King.* Maryknoll, NY: Orbis Books, 2002.

———. *Teilhard de Chardin and Eastern Religions: Spirituality and Mysticism in an Evolutionary World.* New York: Paulist Press, 2011.

Lehninger, Albert. *Principles of Biochemistry*, 2d ed. London: Worth Publishers, 1993.

Lewin, Roger. *Complexity: Life at the Edge of Chaos.* New York: Macmillan, 1992.

Lukas, Mary, and Ellen Lukas. *Teilhard.* Garden City, NY: Doubleday, 1977.

Lyons, J. A. *The Cosmic Christ in Origen and Teilhard de Chardin.* New York: Oxford University Press, 1982.

Merton, Thomas. *Hagia Sophia*. Lexington, KY: Stamperio del Santuccio, 1962.

Mitchell, Melanie. *Complexity: A Guided Tour*. New York: Oxford University Press, 2009.

Mortier, Jeanne, and Marie-Louise Aboux, eds. *Teilhard de Chardin Album*. New York: Harper and Row, 1966.

Nicolis, Gregoire, and Ilya Prigogine, *Exploring Complexity: An Introduction*. New York: W. H. Freeman, 1989.

Ortiz, John M. *The Tao of Music: Sound Psychology: Using Music to Change Your Life*. York Beach, ME: Samuel Weiser, 1997.

Panikkar, Raimon. *Christophany: The Fullness of Man*. Maryknoll, NY: Orbis Books, 2004.

Pickover, Clifford A. *The Loom of God: Mathematical Tapestries at the Edge of Time*. New York: Plenum Publishing, 1997.

Pramuk, Christopher. *Sophia: The Hidden Christ of Thomas Merton*. Collegeville, MN: Liturgical Press, 2009.

Prigogine, Ilya, and Isabelle Stengers. *Order Out of Chaos: Man's New Dialogue with Nature*. New York: Bantam Books, 1984.

Primack, Joel, and Nancy Abrams. *View from the Center of the Universe: Discovering Our Extraordinary Place in the Cosmos*. New York: Riverhead Books, 2006.

Salmon, James, SJ. "Teilhard's Science." In *Rediscovering Teilhard's Fire*, edited by Kathleen Duffy, SSJ. Philadelphia: St. Joseph's University Press, 2010.

Salmon, James, and Nicole Schmitz-Moormann. "Evolution as Revelation of a Triune God." *Teilhard Studies* 46 (Spring 2003).

Sargent, Ted. *The Dance of Molecules: How Nanotechnology Is Changing Our Lives*. New York: Thunder's Mouth Press, 2006.

Schafer, R. Murray. *The Tuning of the World: A Pioneering Exploration into the Past History and Present State of the Most Neglected Aspect of Our Environment: The Soundscape*. New York: Alfred A. Knopf, 1977.

Schef, T. J. M., ed. *Models in Paleobiology*. San Francisco: Freeman, 1972.

Soelle, Dorothee. *The Silent Cry: Mysticism and Resistance*. Minneapolis: Fortress Press, 2001.

Swimme, Brian Thomas, and Mary Evelyn Tucker. *Journey of the Universe*. New Haven, CT: Yale University Press, 2011.

Tarnas, Richard. *The Passion of the Western Mind: Understanding the Ideas That Have Shaped Our World View*. New York: Harmony Books, 1991.

Teilhard de Chardin, Pierre. *Activation of Energy: Enlightening Reflections on Spiritual Energy*. Translated by René Hague. New York: A Harvest Book/Harcourt, 1978.

————. *Building the Earth*. Translated by Nöel Lindsay. Wilkes-Barre, PA: Dimension Books, 1965.

————. *Christianity and Evolution*. Translated by René Hague. New York: Harcourt Brace Jovanovich, 1969.

————. *The Divine Milieu*. New York: Harper and Row, 1960.

————. *The Future of Man*. Translated by Norman Denny. New York: Harper and Row, 1964.

————. *Human Energy*. Translated by J. M. Cohen. New York: Harcourt Brace Jovanovich, 1969.

————. *The Heart of Matter*. Translated by René Hague. New York: Harcourt Brace Jovanovich, 1978.

————. *The Human Phenomenon*. Translated by Sara Appleton-Weber. Portland OR: Sussex Academic Press, 1999.

————. *Hymn of the Universe*. Translated by Simon Bartholomew. New York: Harper and Row, 1961.

————. *Journal: Tome I, August 26, 1915–January 4, 1919*. Unabridged text published by Nicole and Karl Schmitz-Moormann. Paris: Fayard, 1975.

————. *Lettres à Jeanne Mortier*. Paris: Éditions du Seuil, 1984.

————. *Letters to Léontine Zanta*. Introductions by Robert Garric and Henri de Lubac. New York: Harper and Row, 1968.

————. *Letters from a Traveler*. New York: Harper and Row, 1962.

————. *Letters to Two Friends: 1926–1952*. Translated by Helen Weaver, edited by Ruth Nanda Anshen. New York: New American Library, 1967.

————. *The Making of a Mind: Letters from a Soldier-Priest 1941–1919*. Translated by René Hague. New York: Harper and Row, 1965.

————. *Science and Christ*. Translated by René Hague. New York: Harper and Row, 1968.

————. *Towards the Future*. Translated by René Hague. New York: Harcourt Brace Jovanovich, 1975.

————. *The Vision of the Past*. Translated by J. M. Cohen. New York: Harper and Row, 1966.

————. *Writings in Time of War*. Translated by René Hague. New York: Harper and Row, 1968.

Tucker, Mary Evelyn. "Teilhard's Ecological Spirituality." In *Rediscovering Teilhard's Fire*, edited by Kathleen Duffy, SSJ. Philadelphia: St. Joseph's University Press, 2010.

Van Huyssteen, J. Wentzel. *Alone in the World? Human Uniqueness in Science and Theology*. Grand Rapids, MI: Eerdmans, 2006.

Waldrop, M. Mitchell. *Complexity: The Emerging Science at the Edge of Order and Chaos*. New York: Simon and Schuster, 1992.

Wolfram, Stephen. *A New Kind of Science*. Champaign, IL: Wolfram Media, 2002.

Index

Also of Interest from Orbis Books

Teilhard de Chardin
Writings Selected with an Introduction by Ursula King

Modern Spiritual Masters Series
Pierre Teilhard de Chardin (1881-1955) was a French Jesuit theologian and scientist whose visionary writings on the reconciliation of faith and evolutionary theory aroused the suspicions of the Vatican. After his death, the publication of his many books marked him as one of the most influential Catholic thinkers of this century—a mystic whose holistic vision speaks with growing relevance to contemporary spirituality.

ISBN 978-1-57075-248-3 Paperback 160pp.

Spirit of Fire

The Life and Vision of Pierre Teilhard de Chardin
Ursula King

Pierre Teihard de Chardin, Jesuit theologian, mystic, and scientist, was also a prophet in the expanding dialogue between religion, science, and mysticism whose views put him on a collision course with his Jesuit superiors in France and church authorities in Rome. Forbidden to publish his theological writings, he devoted his long and fascinating life to scientific projects around the world. The posthumous publication of *The Divine Milieu, Hymn of the Universe, The Phenomenon of Man* marked Teilhard as one of the most influential Catholic thinkers of the 20th century.

ISBN 978-1-57075-177-6 Paperback 176pp., ills., b/w photos.

Teilhard in the 21st Century: The Emerging Spirit of Earth
Arthur Fabel and Donald St. John, editors

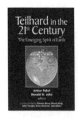

More than fifty years after his death the work of Jesuit Pierre Teilhard de Chardin continues to shape contemporary work in spirituality, theology, and the interaction of science and religion. These essays drawn from *Teilhard Studies* show how this giant of the twentieth century sheds light on the most urgent spiritual challenges of our time. Contributors include Thomas Berry, Brian Swimme, Ursula King, Donald Gray, Thomas King, John Grim and Mary Evelyn Tucker, William Rees, Arthur Fabel, John Haught, Eulalio Balthasar, Eleanor Rae, and Joseph Grau.

ISBN 978-1-57075-507-1 Paperback 254pp.

Available from your bookseller or direct.
Call toll-free 1-800-258-5838 M-F 8-4 ET or
order online www.orbisbooks.com

From Teilhard to Omega
Co-creating an Unfinished Universe
Edited by Ilia Delio, OSF

A landmark effort in the work of evolutionary theology, From Teilhard to Omega *will be of interest to scholars, students, and seekers alike.*

Thirteen leading scholars fulfill Teilhard de Chardin's hope that a future generation apply his learnings to the needs of their age. Each chapter sheds new insight on God and humankind's role in co-creation, and the wisdom we need to forge the future. Most of all, these visionaries inspire us to do our share to advance a spiritual universe. The contributors include: John F. Haught, Edward Vacek, Patrick H. Byrne, Francois Euve, Ilia Delio, Denis Edwards, Kathleen Duffy, Ursula King, and John C. Haughey.

"Ilia Delio has challenged a team of Teilhard experts by asking them, in their fields, to envision how unfinished humanity's convergent journey toward Omega has progressed in complexity and consciousness since Teilhard's day. It's a hope-filled book, exploring Teilhard's realm of the 'not yet,' spilling over with fascinating and prophetic thoughts and images on things to come."
—Louis Savary, Ph.D., S.T.D., author, *The New Spiritual Exercises*

"A useful and much overdue contribution! These wonderfully diverse and helpful essays will open up many new access routes to a Christian mystic whose time has definitely arrived."
—The Rev. Cynthia Bourgeault, Ph.D., author,
The Wisdom Jesus and The Holdy Trinity and the Law of Three

Ilia Delio, OSF, is Director of the Catholic Studies Program and Visiting Professor at Georgetown University, and former Senior Fellow in Science and Religion at Woodstock Theological Center, Georgetown. She is the author of the award-winning books *Christ in Evolution, The Emergent Christ,* and *The Unbearable Wholeness of Being.*

ISBN 978-1-62698-069-3 Paperback 272pp., index
Available from your bookseller or direct.
Call toll-free 1-800-258-5838 M-F 8-4 ET or
order online www.orbisbooks.com